FROM THE GOLD COAST TO ELECTRIC AVENUE

My Life Journey; An autobiography

BY ASHIA FLORENCE COBBLAH

Published by Faunteewrites Limited

© Ashia Florence Cobblah, 2019.

The author asserts the moral right to be identified as the author of this work in accordance with the copyright, designs and patents Act 1988.

All rights reserved. No part of this publication may be reproduced, stored in a retrieval system, or transmitted in any form or by any means - electronic, mechanical, photocopying, recording or otherwise - without the prior permission of the copyright owner.

A CIP catalogue record for this book is available from the British Library.

ISBN: **978 1 913103 00 2**

DEDICATION

"I dedicate this book to the young ladies and women of the world to follow their unique path to be productive and successful in their endeavours"

TABLE OF CONTENTS

Chapter 1
    Ashia Florence Cobblah 4

Chapter 2
    Togo. 18

Chapter 3
    Life in Togo. 25

Chapter 4
    Return to Gold Coast. 28

Chapter 5
    Living and working from Nsawam 31

Chapter 6
    Languages. 34

Chapter 7
    At Night School 37

Chapter 8
    At the Catholic School. 41

Chapter 9
>   Youth League 45

Chapter 10
>   The Independence of Ghana 50

Chapter 11
>   The Union of Independent African States.
>   54

Chapter 12
>   Haile Selassie in Ghana. 57

Chapter 13
>   The Ghanaian Flag. 62

Chapter 14
>   A Dream of Becoming a Nun. 66

Chapter 15
>   AT CFAO 73

Chapter 16
>   77
>   Holidays in Togo 78

Chapter 17
  To Church with Elias. 81

Chapter 18
  My Engagement. 87

Chapter 19
  The Loss of My Job 93

Chapter 20
  A Dream of Becoming an
  Air Hostess 98

Chapter 21
  At the Marketplace 100

Chapter 22
  The Turning Point.. 103

Chapter 23
  Travelling Abroad 107

Chapter 24
  Cumberland Hotel. 114

Chapter 25
  St. Clair's 117

Chapter 26
A Turning Point...................121

Chapter 27
Home Salon Days 124

Chapter 28
Looking for premises..............126

Chapter 29
Brixton Underground 128

Chapter 30
Ashia Hairdressing Salon at 8 Station Arcade, Brixton 133

Chapter 31
Grand Opening of Ashia Hairdressing Salon in 1976.....................138

Chapter 32
VIP Clientele.....................153

Chapter 33
.................................158
Helping my family members.........159

Chapter 34
'A Need for a Bigger/Larger Salon' . . . 162

Chapter 35
Getting Married 165

Chapter 36
New Bigger Salon on Electric Avenue . 171

Chapter 37
Grand Opening of Ashia Hair design Ltd (on Electric Ave.) 175

Chapter 38
Opening Panache Hair salon in Ghana 192

Chapter 39
Making an impact without realising. . . 195

Chapter 40
Memorable Events. 201

Chapter 41
The opening of The Ashia Hairdressing School 214

Chapter 42
The Belgium Students Visit 222

Chapter 43
  The opening of The Wholesale Business
 226

Chapter 44
  My Retirement 230

Chapter 45
  The Ashia Benevolent Foundation (ABF)
 237

Chapter 46
  Poultry and Event business venture in Ghana 246

Chapter 47
  Some Popular Produce from Ghana and the Continent 250

Chapter 48
  Some Popular African Proverbs and Pearls of Wisdom. 257

FOREWORD

It is a pleasure and an honour to assist my beloved Mother to write her Memoir.

From start to finish it was indeed an exciting and humbling experience. My Mother is sharing her life experiences and her unique journey, from where she was born, to getting to know details about the rest of the family and especially my Grandmother, my Mother's mother and their relationships.

From someone who wanted so badly to become a Nun and live in a convent to become a businesswoman instead and to owning her empire and in-turn helping so many people along the way, is fascinating within itself.

The time we spent together drafting this manuscript, I attentively listened to the stages of her life, learning and visualising her growing up, it was extraordinary to hear her experience and the sacrifices she made.

As we daughters and sons grow up, most of us tend to look outside our home for role models and people we admire in the media. I was undoubtedly one of those people until I began to spend more time with my mother, to listen to her, a person who had made great sacrifices.

Hopefully, this will maybe make you consider your Mother or parents who have done their best for you.

I hope this book becomes a catalyst as a reminder for you to write your Mother's or Father's life journey.

I can say today that, my Mother is indeed my Role Model and I am proud of her achievements and her life experiences.

I am thankful for her long life and for me being able to have become a little bit wiser to have this time to get to know her as a remarkable human being.

Happy Mother's Day always.

Disclaimer: *This is a memoir. I have tried to*

remember events and conversations from my memories of them and have made every effort to ensure the information in this book is as accurate as possible.

Chapter 1

Ashia Florence Cobblah

Ashia with baby daughter in Accra, Ghana.

I was born in Accra, the Gold Coast, but my father was from Togo. I am the second-born and only girl from my father's side though he had some boys. From my mother's side, I am the first-born among the five girls she had.

I was born at a time when the country was called the Gold Coast under British rule for the apparent reason of the abundance of gold in my country. The country is known for its Cocoa cultivation and world-renowned peppers. There are other numerous products that the country cultivates and creates which I will mention later.

There were over a hundred of linguistic and cultural groups recorded in Ghana. The major ethnic groups include: The Akan, Evhe, Ga-Adangbe, Guan and Mole-Dagbane. "The subdivisions of each group share a common cultural heritage, history, language and origin."

There are five related ethnic groups in the Ewe Clan: The Fon, Gen, Phla, Phera and the Aja people. A part of a cluster of related languages commonly called Gbe also spoken in Benin and Ghana. My family is originally from the Evhe clan. It is also known and written as Eve or Ewe.

The Akans are the most extensive collection of people in Ghana with several subgroups and the most populous group being the Ashantes then, the Fantes, Akuapems, Nzemas, Akyems and others, making the Akan language the most popular of Twi and Fanti.

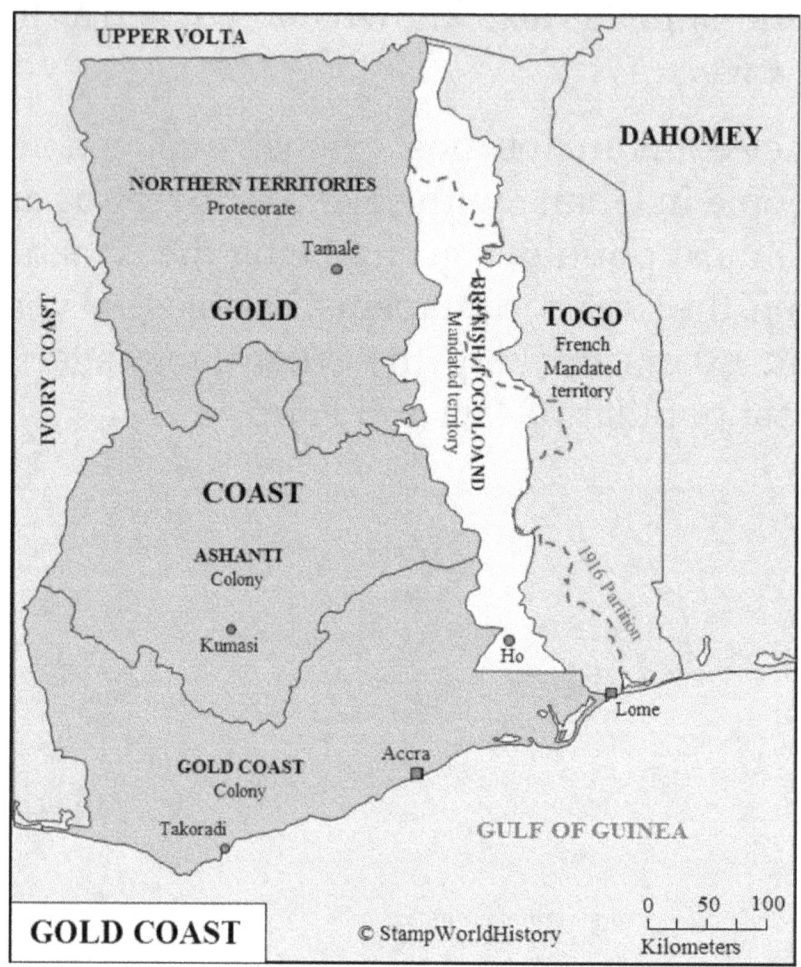

Map of Gold Coast, now known as Ghana

There are approximately 4.8 million people residing in Ghana and Togo in West Africa, who had spread mainly between the Mono and the Volta rivers within the borders of Ghana, Togo and Benin. According to some historians, the Evhes were thought to have migrated from Tando, in modern-day Western Nigeria to Notsie in Togo.

Notsie became the last settlement before migrating and settling in the current place, to Eʋeawó or Eʋenyigba, and settled in the South-Eastern coastal plains of Togo and The Volta Region. As the country is near the sea, it was easy for foreigners to get there by boat and ship.

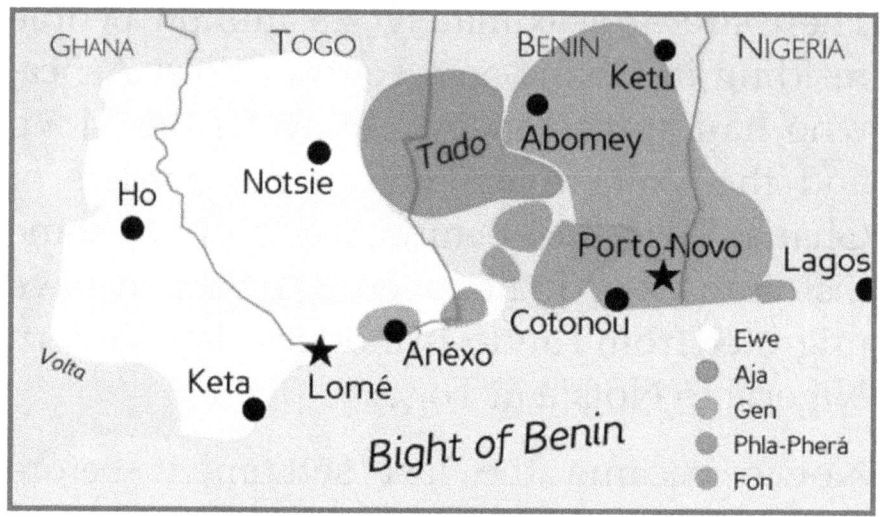

Map of Evhe settlement

I had known about the Portuguese being the first 'visitors' from the 14th century before the British invaders took control of the country and it became known as The Gold Coast.

I recall the elders used to talk about the great kingdoms that had existed from the ancient times as some people who had travelled around Africa and other places came back and told us the stories. We heard about some of The Empires: Dahomey, Mali, Zimbabwe, Songhai, Kongo, Ghana-Kumbi, Zulu, the kingdom of Axum, Buganda and Burundi. Moreover, closer to home was the Asantee Kingdom of the Akan with abundance of Gold.

Royal Ashanti Queen Mother & Warrior Yaa Asantewaa of The Asante Empire in Military Regalia

The story of Nana Yaa Asantewaa, also known as the 'Warrior Queen', is a legendary and empowerment for women across our country. Therefore she is one of my heroes and my role models. After hearing her life story, I was fascinated and excited about this remarkable woman. The Queen Mother was known for her strength and power to have led the Ashanti wars known as the 'War of the Golden Stool' against the injustice of the British invaders. Though she died in exile in Seychelles in 1921, eventually her remains were brought back to her land for a royal burial. Queen Mother, Yaa Asantewaa's life story shall always be in our memories. It's a delight to know there is a museum, a school and a community centre named after her.

The African Society of Polygamy

In some African cultures, including parts of Ghana, polygamy is normal, so my father had two wives. In most parts of Africa, a man can marry as many wives as he can afford. I don't know much about the war, but when I was a little girl, I used to hear the elders saying, "because of the effects of previous wars between clans, we have lost a lot of men, and women became more numerous than the men population."

We had always fought between each other, tribal wars were not uncommon. They were honourable acts, as you represented your tribe during the war. No one was put in chains or treated less of a human being but most importantly, despite our differences, we lived alongside each other in harmony and we inter-married between clans and tribes.

My grandfather, who was a herbalist and Cocoa farmer named Fofo (Father) Ameyibo from my mother's side, was an Assistant Chief "O'Tchami" near Asamankese and Sekondi-Takoradi, the Eastern region of South Ghana.

Fofo received an expansive land and he in-turn created a new striving community village known as, Adiembra, which means, 'good omens should come'. He planted a large amount of cocoa and at the same time was curing the sick and kept his people healthy with herbs and plants. Fofo had four wives and several children including twins. My mother was his first-born.

<u>Map of Ghana showing Asamankese and National Parks and Rivers</u>

My grandfather had wanted some of his children to continue the crafts of herbalism but his children including my mother were not interested because she had her children to care for. It takes years as an understudy to be able to assist my grandfather to learn thousands of plants, herbs and spices and their medicinal uses. He used to complain that *"the young people are not as patient to learn, they had preferred to go to the city and get a 'modern' office or government job."*

My youngest sister Paulina was born in Adiembra, a rural community, which is approximately four hours from Accra. She got christened in Asamankese, the city centre of Adiembra, the business centre of the area.

I recall, during the colonial days, the British had heard of my grandfather. One day, some English men came to visit him and wanted to employ him to manage The Korle-Bu Hospital to treat the sick with herbs. They also wanted him to teach them about the use of a variety of herbs. Fofo declined because he said as the O'Tchami of a community, he had several wives and numerous children to take care of and had several sick people to treat. He rather advised them on who could help. I didn't know of my mother's mother, but I knew my father's mother, who lived in Togo.

Chapter 2

Togo.

Togo is a West African country bordered by Ghana to the West, Benin to the east and Burkina Faso to the north. Like most of other African countries, Togo is also famous with waterfalls, festivals and their mountains and lush greenery.

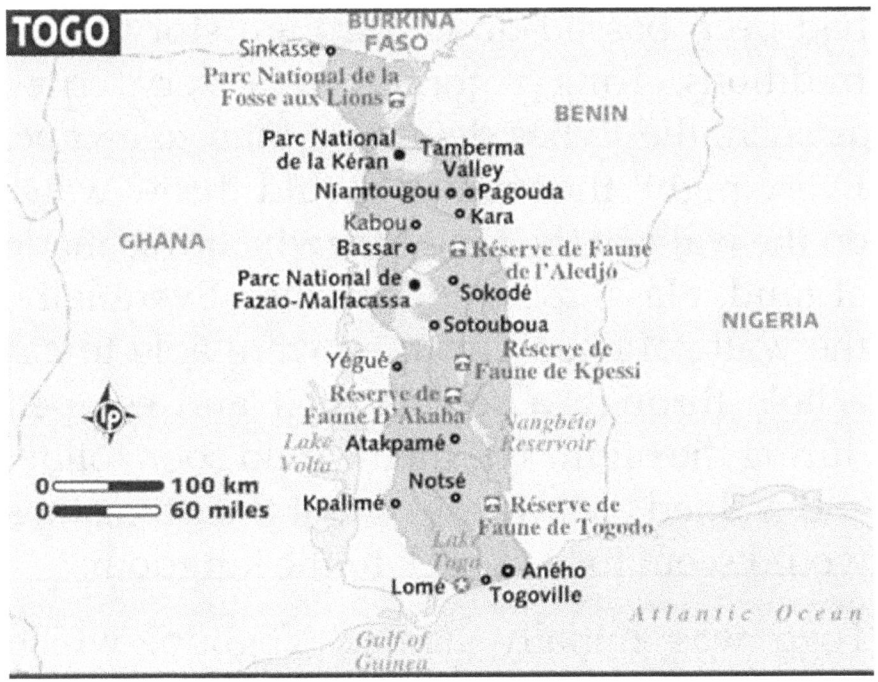

Detailed Map of Togo.

According to our oral history, as children, we were told that the Evhes settled first at Notsie in Togo and then moved to south-eastern Ghana due to the cruelty of the reign of King Agorkoli.

The Evhes went through several many exoduses which began in the 11th century and finally settled as the present-day Evhes in Togo, Ghana and Benin from 15th to 17th century. According to our oral stories that had been passed down through storytelling traditions, King Agorkoli was very cruel; as such, the Evhes devised a plan to escape. Every night, the women would throw water on the walls of the kingdom which was made of mud, glass, rock, and thorns. Eventually, the wall softened and they were able to cut a hole through a section of it and escaped during the night. The men would soon follow and walked backwards so that their footsteps would seem to lead back to the kingdom.

Togo was initially named Togodo, which means 'behind the lake' in the Evhe language, a language derived from Evegbe. My clan was mainly in the fishing and farming trade, but due to the erratic rainfall pattern of the area, it made fishing a highly seasonal and precarious occupation. Therefore, some families were forced to venture into other viable economic and commercial activities such as; trading, weaving clothes and baskets among other trades to survive.

I heard the story that the Germans couldn't pronounce 'Togodo', so it was shortened to Togo. Following the abolition of slavery, the country became a German protectorate from 1884. During the period, it was generally known as the 'scramble for Africa'. The colony was established as part of what was previously known as the Slave Coast.

After the treaty was signed in 1884 with a local King Mlapa, the Germans named their colony 'Togoland'. They developed the country extensively and also profited from the natural resources. It became Germany's only self-supporting colony because of its extensive rail and road infrastructure.

Togoland was known as Germany's model

possession but in the long run, the Togolese didn't appreciate the Germans' brutal *'pacification'* campaigns. At the outbreak of the First World War in 1914, the colony was drawn into the conflict. Togo was quickly overrun by British and French military forces during the 'Togoland Campaign' and placed it under their military rule on, 8th August 1914.

In 1916, during the bitter struggle, The League of Nations, Togoland was split between France and Britain administrative zones – a controversial move which was formalised in 1922 with the creation of British Togoland and French Togoland, a move that divided the population of Evhes.

Apart from the severe and numerous consequences of this division and partitions, one funny joke was the reality among the Evhes that we realised that a family's home would be in French Togoland but their bathroom would be in British Togoland.

Following a 1956 vote, British Togoland was incorporated with the 'Gold Coast'. This is one of the reasons there are significant numbers of Evhes living in Ghana up to this day.

French Togoland gained full independence in 1960 under the country's first president, Sylvanus Olympio. He was an Evhe from the south and appeared to disregard the interests of the northerners. He was assassinated in a coup in 1963 by soldiers from the north.

The second president of Togo was Nicolas Grunitzky, from 1963 to 1967. He had a German father and a Togolese mother. He also happened to be president Olympio's brother-in-law.

Grunitzky attempted to unify the country by including several political parties in his government. He was, however, toppled in a bloodless military coup led by then sergeant, Gnassingbe Eyadema, a Northerner. Togo unfortunately, was the first African country to experience a military coup following independence. General Eyadema was the President from 1967 until his death in 2005. His son Faure, who had been the country's former minister of public works, mines and telecommunications was named the president. After international pressure and re-election, he was finally sworn into power in 2005 until this day.

Chapter 3

Life in Togo

I lived in Accra with my mother, Mary Ameyibo, who was affectionately called 'Mami Yaa'- meaning born on Thursday. We lived with my three sisters (one had already passed away).

I started school at the age of five but about the age of seven, my mother decided to send me to Togo to spend time with my father and grandmother. I don't recall going to school during the three years I spent in Togo. I learnt to speak Evhe, the native language of Togo.

My father's name was Constantine Kobblah Atiagbo, a coffee farmer and a carpenter. He left me a plot of coffee when he died. My father attended a German-run school in Togo and I was told my grandfather also attended the same school.

The Germans seemed to have done a lot in Togo: the building of roads, hospitals and schools. They had also introduced the

Presbyterian religion and built churches. My mother was a Presbyterian like most Ghanaians at the time.

During the ancient time, in the African tradition, we believed only in oral tradition and information was passed down from generation to generation.

Some information were regarded as sacred. This was the main reason some of the Kings and Chiefs were against writing things down. The Germans helped scribe the Evhe language to help produce a dictionary and bible in the Evhe language.

Chapter 4

Return to Gold Coast

At the age of ten, my mother came to Togo to take me back to Accra, the Gold Coast, to join my sisters: Veronica, Pauline and Felicia. My mother was a celebrated Accra trader, selling household goods, as in those days the markets were prominent places to buy and sell products before shops and supermarkets became the norm.

My mother had a friend, Mrs. Arthur. ('Wawawa' as we affectionately called her) She was a cake baker, who was looking for girls to sell her cakes in Nsawah. My mother arranged for me and one of my sisters to pick up the cakes and retail at The Nsawah Train Station every morning. So, at the age of thirteen, I started learning the business of selling cakes.

It is interesting to note that Mrs. Arthur's name is apparently an English surname and she was married to a Fanti man. Like a lot of people from the Fanti clan, they had adopted the surnames from the English during the colonial era. I am not sure why, but one reason could be that they had lived closest to the coast when the ships first arrived. So, they were more accommodating and closest to the English.

Chapter 5

Living and working from Nsawam

Wawawa's family was transferred from Nsawam to Accra because of her husband's job as a trainmaster. She then asked my mother if I could come and live with her. My mother agreed. Then I went to live with her in Accra.

Wawawa used to call me Akosua instead of Ashia because Akosua means Sunday-born in Fanti language and she wanted people to recognise me as one of her daughters. My name Ashia has different meanings as well as Sunday-born in the Ga language of Accra.

I recall when I visited my Father in Togo, some families in the community said they liked my name, so a few named their girls Ashia and two of my uncles named their daughters Ashia too.

From The Gold Coast To Electric Avenue

Map of The Volta Region of Ghana

Chapter 6

Languages

Working on the trains, I came across different types of people and from that, I learnt to speak different languages. Apart from speaking the Evhe and Ga languages, I learnt to be fluent in Twi and Fanti dialects of the Akan languages because, there were numerous dialects. I also learnt to speak basic Hausa, the language of the Nigerian Muslims living in the north of Accra and Yoruba from Nigerians living in and around Accra.

During the time I was living with Wawawa, I learnt how to bake various types of pancakes and Ghanaian doughnuts called Boflot, popularly known as 'Puff-Puff. I baked and sold cakes until I was fifteen years then Wawawa decided to enrol me into a night school to learn English and Mathematics. It was okay because I was reluctant to attend day-time school due to my cake selling job. But I found out that it was easier to fry and sell doughnuts which I used to sell in the markets.

I started selling on the trains, travelling from Accra to Koforidua. I would leave by 7 a.m. and return by 5 p.m., Mondays to Saturdays.

The phenomenon of Language sharing in Likpe-Volta Region.

I recall a fascinating experience when I visited the Volta, one of Ghana's numerous regions and a small community called Likpe. The people speak Evhe until midday and after midday they change to talk in Twi! I found a real sense of unity and sharing of cultures through speaking each other's language.

Chapter 7

At Night School

At the age of 16, I returned to live with my mother while also attending night classes which was a free course. The school master at the night-school saw my grades and urged me to attend day-time school because I achieved high marks and was in his own words, 'clever.'

I was reluctant to attend day school because it was expensive, and it meant that I had to stop selling doughnuts but for the insistence of the school master, a Sierra-Leonean. He had a meeting with my mother and she explained that she cannot afford the school fees, uniforms and books. The school master offered to cover everything if my mother would agree for me to attend day-time school.

I started to attend day-time school while living with my mother. The school time was from 8 a.m. to 2pm and I would then go and sell daily provisions like sugar, milk etc. during the week-days. I began to sell these daily provisions by approaching a local businessman Mr. Kodjoe who had a supermarket and I asked him if I could sell some of his items for him and he agreed without asking me any details of where I lived. He trusted me and gave me some items to sell every afternoon, after school.

When I finished selling the things, I would then return to the shop to hand in the money and he would give me a percentage from that. This was my afternoon job for about two years.

During my mid-teens, I sat for The National Entry Exam which I passed and then I started attending a catholic school. I attended for three years and during that time, I would wake up at 2 a.m., every morning to fry doughnuts and sell at the sea-side especially to the fishermen for their lunch before going to school. I sold at the seaside every day and even sometimes the fishermen used to give me some fish to take home to my mother. Every evening as well, I would sell sweets, biscuits, matches and single cigarettes which I had obtained from Mr. Kodjoe to sell to passers-by going to the cinema. I sold these items outside our house-gate because it was convenient and safe until 10 p.m. It was a common practice for some people to sell items in front of their homes. On Sundays, I would attend church and afterwards, I would rest and do my school homework.

During all this time, my mother had been unwell, and she hadn't been able to work, so I had become the sole breadwinner: paying our rent, managing the household and taking care of the family.

Chapter 8

At the Catholic School

When I started attending catholic school, I started to consider my career-path seriously. I had thought of becoming a Nun or a Reverend Sister because I liked the quietness of their lives. Unlike most young ladies, I didn't have time for parties or boys.

At school, I was quiet and kept to myself. I didn't have time for friends or girly-talks, as my mother was ill and I was looking after the whole family: paying all the bills. I had a business mindset from a young age and I spent a lot of time thinking about how to budget and manage.

I was given a name at school, 'walk alone' for not trying to socialise or have any friends. One day my Domestic-Science teacher, Mrs. Atiogbe noticed my anti-social behaviour and asked me why I don't walk around with any friends. I told her that I didn't want to and didn't have time for friends. She advised me not to ever say that again as it is not right to say such a thing. I apologised to her for saying that.

I loved attending school but my only problem was lateness, as I was always rushing to school after selling. I was always in trouble and getting punished, usually to do gardening for being late.

One day my class teacher Mrs. Awadzie asked one of my classmates if she knew why I was always late and she told her that I sell at the sea-side before coming to school.

Mrs. Awadzie requested that I should come to her house on Sunday. She asked me to explain to her why I was always late. So, I told her that my mother was unwell and I was the sole breadwinner for our household and that I wake up by 2 a.m. to fry and sell doughnuts at the sea-side and in the evenings, I sold snacks on a table outside our home too.

My teacher started to cry and she asked me why I hadn't told her as she had been punishing me for lateness. She understood the reason, so she stopped my punishments. I was glad my teacher knew the reason for my lateness and was very happy also that was no longer punished for it.

Surprisingly, I loved running. I was the only runner in my class who was competing against the other classes. I used to win prizes from the Sisters of the School. That was the highlight for me at my school.

Chapter 9

Youth League

I was one of the main orators at the Youth League Conference.

In my late teens, I heard about our president, Kwame Nkrumah doing something for the youths of Ghana, so I got interested and went and joined the party. President Kwame Nkrumah's party was called The Convention

People's Party (CPP). It was a socialist political party based on the ideas of our first President of Ghana.

The CPP was formed in June 1949 to campaign for the independence of the country. Its slogan was "Forward Ever, Backward Never". I thought it was very positive. I became a member of the CPP's Youth League, which promoted good governance and for a better lifestyle for the youths of Ghana. The president realised the importance of young people as the future of the country.

I was one of the leading orators at the Youth League Conference therefore, during the party's conference I would recite President Nkrumah's speech word-for-word.

I recall seeing some of my classmates in the audience with their parents. I knew they must have been shocked to see me, someone who was usually very quiet at school now on the stage reciting the President's speech.

Incidentally, I was reported to my school Principal for getting involved in politics which was being rebellious. I was given a warning not to be involved in politics.

However, I stayed connected with the Youth League and continued because it was educational and exciting as we got to go on day-trips to other towns around Ghana but I was extra careful not to get another warning.

I was an essential key member for the Youth League and Mr. E.C. Quaye known as "Kakabuka," the Chairman was like a father to me. He asked other members and I to travel for three days to Nkroful, in Nzema to organise a Youth League group. It was a town in the Western Region, located near Axim, where he was born.

The members I was privileged to travel with were Mr. J.E. Djantuah –a government Minister, our secretary, Mr. S.S. Badu, and Beatrice, a youth member.

We went to meet Mrs. Hannah Kodjo who would help to set-up and galvanise the league of youths in the town. We stayed for three days and I was the main speaker to promote the

Youth League group. It was a great success as we had managed to get a lot of youths signed-up with the agreement of their parents.

Mr. E. C. Quaye was a very influential figure in my life after my own father had died. He was a prominent figure during The Gold Coast era, as he was the first Major of Ghana from 1961 to 1964.

I didn't have any other father-figure in my life until I met Mr. Quaye in the Youth League. As he was the chairman of the Youth League, I got to know him very well as he was directing the League. I met his whole family and even one of his children was also named Florence.

He treated me as and called me one of his daughters. I felt very comforted. His wife, a prominent woman in the Ghanaian society was also like a second mother to me. I stayed as an active member until I started working.

After a few years, the Youth League was dissolved, and a new party called YMP for 'The Young Pioneer Movement' was formed.

Chapter 10

The Independence of Ghana

Dr Kwame Nkrumah. The first Prime Minister and President of the Republic of Ghana

After the Independence in March 1957, Ghana became the very first African nation to become independent of European colonisation.

Our first elected President Kwame Nkrumah renamed the country, The Republic of Ghana, post-colonialism. Kwame Nkrumah commenced his political career as the Prime Minister of Ghana, under colonial rule.

Kwame Nkrumah's heritage came from the Akan/Ashantee Clan. His father was a goldsmith and he often worked with his father. According to the naming customs of Akan Clan, his name Kwame, meant born on a Saturday.

Shortly after the country's independence, on 31st December 1957, he married a North African, an Egyptian, Fathia Halen Ritzk.

It was a double celebration for most Ghanaians and Egyptians and Ghana loved her as their first lady.

One of the reasons he married a woman from another African country was, according to his famous quote and vision, *"Africa Must Unite"*, meaning, if all African countries unite then the continent will progress. He hoped his marriage would inspire the nations and the governments to unite.

His famous speech regarding unity was, *"It is clear that we must find an African solution to our problems, and this can only be found in African Unity, Africa could become one of the greatest forces for good in the world."*

Chapter 11

The Union of Independent African States.

In 1958, President Nkrumah of Ghana collaborated with President Ahmed Sekou Toure of Guinea to develop a common currency and unify foreign policies.

The flag which represented the union of the three independent African States: Ghana, Guinea, Mali.

They joined forces to form the Union of African States. In 1960, President Keita Modibo of Mali joined the alliance, which established The Ghana-Guinea-Mali Union. A famous Ghanaian singer, E.T. Mensah created a song about the alliance. The song titled, "Ghana-Guinea-Mali" was very popular and built a strong understanding of the unity of Africa. Till this day, I still remember the song. This was a short-lived legacy of the practice of Pan-Africanism in my lifetime.

Chapter 12

Haile Selassie in Ghana

His Imperial Majesty Haile Selassie I of Ethiopia visiting Ghana with Dr Kwame Nkrumah, after landing from EAL Airline, 1960

When His Imperial Majesty Haile Selassie of Ethiopia visited Ghana, December 1st -5th 1960, it was a big affair and crucial to President Nkrumah. He had great admiration for the country and their people.

Ethiopia derived prestige from its uniquely successful military resistance during the late 19th century as the only African country to defeat European colonial power and to retain its Sovereignty. Ethiopia was the most admired African country across the continent and beyond.

His Imperial Majesty Haile Selassie I and Dr. Kwame Nkrumah, 1960

Apparently, when the delegates arrived from Ethiopia, President Nkrumah selected a young man called Papa Yeboah who was from my home district to guide and assist the Emperor during his state visit in Ghana. When Papa got home, he mentioned he was so excited and astonished to have met the H.I.M Selassie.

He said that Emperor Selassie was an unusual man because he didn't like to put on any artificial lights while in his room as he preferred natural light. Interestingly, the name 'Selasi' is also used in Evhe Language as a first name for women. It means, "God has heard it" or "the hearer has heard it."

In 1931, Kwame Nkrumah was made headmaster of the school in Axim, a town in Nzima, Ghana, where he founded The Nzima Literacy Society. Ironically, the town Axim reminds me of the town of Axum in Ethiopia: a town in the city of the Northern part of Ethiopia, which is one of the oldest continuously, inhabited places in Africa. In ancient times, there was the Kingdom of Axum. Is **Axum and Axim, a coincidence**?

Chapter 13

The Ghanaian Flag.

Before the arrival of Europeans, we didn't need flags. Africans did not believe in the division of lands. When the Europeans arrived, the Elders noticed there were European flags being placed in the areas which they took control of. It was a strange sight for the natives.

After Ghana's independence in 1957, the President commissioned and appointed Theodosia Salome Okoh to design our flag.

She was a Ghanaian Stateswoman, a teacher and an artist.

Ghana, being the first African independent nation, the design of the flag influenced other African country flags. The design of the Flag of Ghana was symbolic. It was designed to emulate the flag of The Ethiopian Empire to feature the Red, Gold and Green colours which were also recognised as the Pan-African colours. The red represents the blood of those who died in the country's struggle for independence from the British, the gold represents the mineral wealth of the country, the green symbolises the country's rich forests and natural wealth while the black star is the symbol of African emancipation.

Interestingly, the black star in the centre was also considered to be linked to the Black Star Line, a shipping line incorporated by the Jamaican born Marcus Garvey which, operated from 1919 to 1922. President Nkrumah was an avid reader and supporter of Marcus Garvey. The Ghana national football team is nationally known as the Black Stars.

Presently, in Ghana, we have The Black Star Square in Accra also known as Independence Square, a public square which holds the Accra Stadium as well as the Kwame Nkrumah Memorial, for him and his wife.

Coat of Arms of Ghana

Chapter 14

A Dream of Becoming a Nun

At the age of 20, I had completed my standard education at a Catholic School, and I had managed to convert my family from Presbyterians to Catholics, and we all started attending mass together.

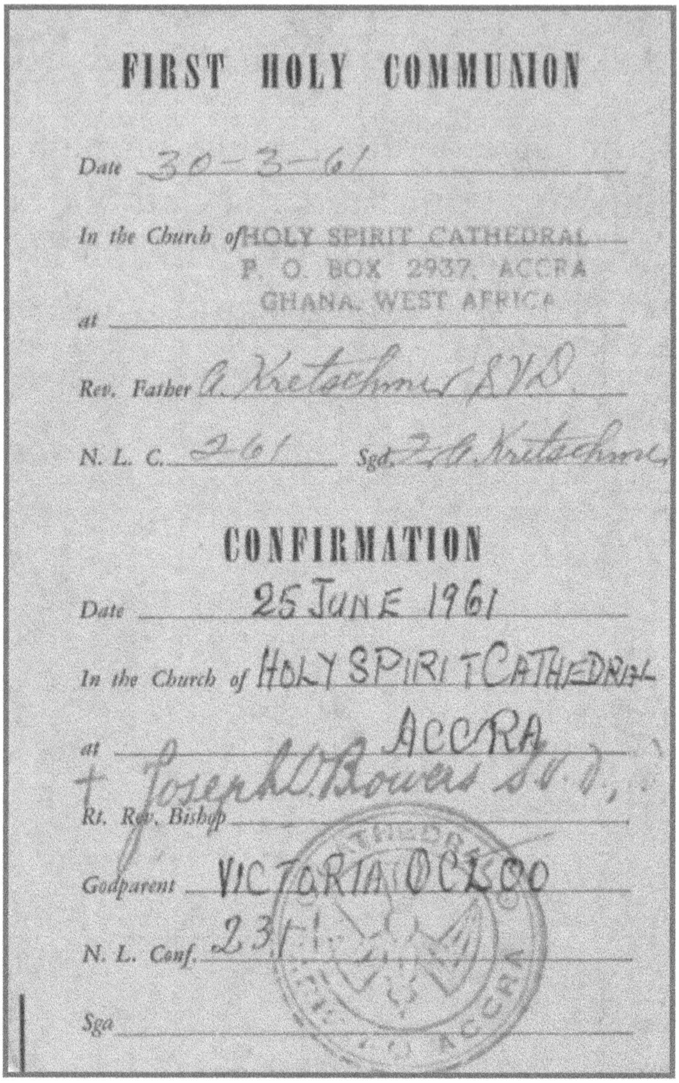

FIRST HOLY COMMUNION

Date: 30-3-61

In the Church of HOLY SPIRIT CATHEDRAL
P. O. BOX 2937, ACCRA
GHANA, WEST AFRICA

Rev. Father A. Kretschmer SVD

N. L. C. 261   Sgd. A. Kretschmer

CONFIRMATION

Date: 25 JUNE 1961

In the Church of HOLY SPIRIT CATHEDRAL

at ACCRA

Rt. Rev. Bishop † Joseph O. Bowers SVD

Godparent: VICTORIA OCLOO

N. L. Conf. 23

Sga

On the 30th of March 1961, I had my first Holy Communion and my confirmation as a Catholic on the 25th June 1961.

The lady who signed my confirmation card as a witness was Victoria Ocloo. I believe she is related to one of our national heroes, Esther Afua Ocloo, a Ghanaian entrepreneur and pioneer. She was the co-founder of Women's World Banking (WWB), a global micro-lending organisation. She was affectionately known as 'Auntie Ocloo' and was the first to set up a food canning business in the country. It was used to overcome prejudice against locally produced goods and to highlight 'Made-in-Ghana' goods in 1958 and it was encouraged by our Prime Minister Kwame Nkrumah. 'Auntie Ocloo' later became a role-model for me.

I was seriously considering my career-path to become a nun. This type of life had really appealed to me, as it had a calming type of experience. I wanted to stay and live in a convent to have a peace and quiet life as well as to pray for mankind. I was strongly attracted to this way of life and it suited my personality and temperament. I had enrolled earlier at The Accra Polytechnic to study typing for 2 years.

<u>Accra Polytechnic School logo, where I attended</u>

During my study, I had decided to start attending classes at the church to become a reverend sister. I had not mentioned my plans to my mother. She only found out when the priest sent the elders to visit her at our house to notify and get her permission for me to become a nun. Unfortunately, my mother started crying and refused. The elders left without getting her permission.

After the elders had left, my mother came upstairs and continued crying. She asked me 'why I have to do this to her knowing that I'm the only one supporting her and what do I expect her to do and how is she going to survive without me'? I continued attending the Nunnery class.

However, a letter was sent to our home from the bishop of Accra, Bishop Joseph Oliver Bowers, who was a Caribbean from Dominica, the first African-Caribbean Bishop of the Gold Coast colony as all previous bishops in Ghana had been of European origin. He notified my mother that I have been accepted into the convent and she didn't speak to me for a few days because she was upset.

My mother went to see Reverend Father A. Kretschmer, our local priest with the letter to beg him not to allow me to become a Nun as I was her only 'eyes and helper'. She then threatened the priest that she will go to Togo and get the 'Gendarmerie' to arrest him if he accepts me as a Nun. What was funny was that she didn't believe in the Accra policemen but in her own view, the Togolese-French policemen as being stronger and more fearful!

The priest chuckled but realised the seriousness of the situation as my mother's only helper and she was also unwell and couldn't cope without me. She also cried that her life would be 'over' without me. The priest told her that he will have a meeting with the elders and let her know of their decision.

Considering all these reasons, the priest sadly declined my quest to become a Nun.

Chapter 15

AT CFAO

After completing the Typing & Shorthand Course, I then attended The National Cash Register College (NCR) for a year to study Machinery to gain an NCR Diploma.

I, as a working woman wearing the latest Ghanaian pattern design called "Kwame Nkrumah's pen in 1965

After graduating, I approached Mr. E.C. Quaye, who was like a father to me to let him know that I had completed my course. He said he will look out for a job for me.

After a few months, he called me to come and get an application form for the Compagnie Française de l'Afrique Occidentale (CFAO) office. It was a French multi-national company with offices around the world. Within a few months, I was offered a position. I was a machine operator in the Accounting Department of CFAO based in Accra. Approximately, after one year, I was given the task of training new operators, mainly from Nigeria and other African countries.

I felt my life had a purpose: my mother was doing well, my sisters were doing fine and all the bills were being paid.

During my lunch breaks, I would go and buy lunch and one day after a year, I noticed a Portuguese shop selling materials and I thought of purchasing some cotton materials to sell to my colleagues. At work, my male colleagues were really interested in buying materials to make shirts from the materials. It became very popular and the news spread throughout the company. I was supplying a lot of materials to many of my colleagues and we had an agreement to pay at the end of the month. It became very successful and useful to them as it saves them time to go out and purchase materials. It was a profitable side-business for me.

Many Ghanaians got excited by foreign goods and products to the point of nearly making our own goods become obsolete. We had an ancient natural dental plant commonly referred to as chewing stick. This benefited oral health and hygiene. We also had a dental sponge that was usually used to keep the teeth and gums clean and healthy. Regrettably, numerous amounts of English manufactured goods flooded the country and diminished the use of our national products.

However, what became a comical sight in the early morning was to see people brushing their teeth outside their compounds because they were proud to be seen using foreign products such as the toothbrush and toothpaste.

My favourite hobby was dancing, especially ballroom dancing including; Waltz, Slow-trot and Quick-Step. I thought that this was one good thing the English brought over which was beneficial to me. I would attend dancing on some Saturdays, and when I wasn't dancing, I would prefer to be at home sleeping. My usual day would be: to finish work at 4.30 p.m., to get home by 5pm, eat and shower and then be in bed by 6.30 p.m. Unfortunately, I wasn't like my sisters. I didn't enjoy going to the cinema and attending parties. I was thrilled and successful at CFAO as a machine operator and a trainer. I did this for four years.

Chapter 16

Holidays in Togo

A Togolese family was living near our house in Accra and the young man in the family called Andre Atikpo became very close to my mother. She mentioned to him that we will be visiting Togo soon. Andre wrote a letter to be given to his uncle called Elias Ocloo, who worked at the Post Office in the city, Lomé.

When we got to Lomé, a few days later, my mother instructed me to deliver the letter to Elias at the Post Office. When I got there, I then asked for Elias. The receptionist informed him that there was a visitor for him. I introduced myself and explained who the letter was from. Elias opened the letter and he briefly read it. I did not know the content of the message. As I was about to leave, he kindly asked if I could wait for a few minutes. I agreed as it was not an issue.

He then ordered a taxi to escort me to our

house, so he could greet and thank my mother. In the early evening, by surprise, Elias came to visit us after work to chat with my mother. Three days later, he came again to visit us and requested if we could visit his family for a dinner and to meet his wife.

My mother and I attended the dinner and met his wife, Beatrice.

Elias's house was large and spacious. We had a lovely evening. Beatrice was very welcoming and the food was excellent. We also met their children. During our stay, we also visited some of our relatives outside the city. We then returned to Ghana.

Chapter 17

To Church with Elias

On our return, a few months later, Andre invited Elias to Ghana for a weekend. He came to greet us at our home on a Saturday evening. He then asked us what we would be doing on Sunday. My mother told him that we would be going to church and he requested to join us.

Sunday morning, he came early and waited for us. The three of us went to church together. As Elias was impeccably dressed in a classic French style suit, some of my friends noticed the visitor with us and after church, they gathered to greet him. They were whispering questions and comments asking; "Who is this impeccably dressed stranger?" He didn't dress and look like a Ghanaian. The other surprise was that they had never seen me walking with a man!

The situation continued as we were walking past the Methodist church where I also have friends. Some of them rushed up to me to ask about the stranger and also asked to be introduced.

I was so embarrassed because I have never received so much attention like this before. Luckily my mother was very helpful and managed the situation. I couldn't wait to get out of the position. I noticed Elias behaved like a gentleman and enjoyed the favourable attention. My mother invited him to our home for lunch and same evening he left for Togo.

When he was leaving, he asked my mother if I could visit Togo because his wife Beatrice wanted me to attend a function they would be participating in two weeks' time. My mother agreed. When the time came, I travelled to Lomé and stayed with them.

My mother liked Elias very much and started to call him her 'son'. Elias politely asked that I call him by his first name, Elias, rather than being formal.

The 'function' turned out to be a trip to the cinema and dinner. During my stay, I spent a lot of time with Beatrice. She was very friendly and took me many places.

She made me feel welcomed and called me her sister. She then invited me to come to stay anytime I am on holiday in Togo. The gesture was very nice, as I didn't usually go out in Ghana. I liked Togo very much because it was different from Ghana. There was a slower-pace with holiday feels to it. It was also a smaller country than Ghana. Togo had been a French colony, so the national language for business, commerce and education is French while the local indigenous language spoken by the majority is Evhe. It is unlike Ghana which is a bigger country with numerous languages and dialects.

Togo seemed to be treated as a holiday destination and the beach was most famous for French foreigners and expatriates. The Togolese local dishes are slightly different in taste because they have and use more variety of spices which I realised when Madame Beatrice took me to the markets for shopping. I learnt to cook Togolese dishes using their spices and herbs. I realised that Togolese women were very extravagant with their spices and creative with their dishes. Madame Beatrice taught me how to cook Togolese dishes by assisting her in the kitchen. As Togo is 'next door' to Ghana, we do have similar recipes.

Elias was showing a lot of interest in me and I didn't understand the attention as he was married and with children. I told him that I had taken a vow of chastity with my church. Therefore, I must go and notify my priest.

Madame Beatrice was very attentive and kind to me. I was also fond of her and she told me that she would be delighted if I could be her 'sister-wife'. She insisted I called her Sister instead of Madame. I was astonished and confused that she would like me to be her husband's wife. It is a custom in Africa that a man can have as many wives as he can afford.

When I got back to Ghana, I spoke with my mother and she was so thrilled with the idea. I made an appointment to meet my priest and he was overjoyed that I have finally found someone. He then revoked the chastity vow.

On the third visit, I became pregnant. When I notified Elias, he was overjoyed and he asked me when I could return to Togo so that he could propose to me and announce our engagement. Some men before they marry they would check that the woman wasn't barren as children were very important. My mother was also happy that her Ashia was finally pregnant. She was rejoicing around the house.

Chapter 18

My Engagement

<u>An engagement photo with Elias.</u>

Elias invited me and my family to Togo to celebrate the pregnancy and our engagement. Then he presented a ring to me. I used to spend some of my weekends in Togo.

When I was about to give birth, I asked for my maternity leave for three months. I was in Togo when the contractions started, so I gave birth in Togo as Elias desperately wanted. It was a natural and uncomplicated delivery. It was also a miracle that I gave birth to a girl on his birthday, the 21st July which was also a Saturday.

Elias wanted the baby to be named after him, as Elise. I refused because he had not named any of his other children after him. I didn't want any animosity and jealousy in the family. He eventually understood and agreed with the female version of Victor as Victoire or Victorine. Victorine was internationally easier to pronounce so we decided to take it.

Elias revealed to me that he was a wealthy and prominent man in the community because he had other businesses and ventures apart from working at the Post Office. Elias then confessed to me he had another wife named Fortune who also had children with him. He explained that if he had mentioned her at the beginning, he was afraid I would have refused him. So, he had three women to take care of.

For the next few weeks, I spent time resting with Victorine in Togo after the birth. Sister Beatrice was a great help and my mother was coming back and forth from Ghana to Togo. At the end of my maternity leave, I returned to Ghana with Victorine to continue work. I managed to find an au-pair to look after Victorine while I was at work.

Three generations of my family; myself on the right side of my Mother, Mary Ameyibo also known as "Mami Yaa" holding her granddaughter Victorine.

When Victorine was about three years old, I was pregnant with my second child. I gave birth again to a baby girl in Ghana, who we named Doreen. I then returned to work in Ghana. Unfortunately, after a year she died. The loss was tough to deal with so I took time off work to recuperate.

Chapter 19

The Loss of My Job

A turning point came when I decided to help a person who was searching for a job. A visiting refugee from Dahomey (now called Benin) was visiting a relative who happened to live in our compound which was a communal space with several houses. It also had a big wall around it to provide protection. The man had spoken to my mother to know if I could help his relative, Mr. Duwa who fled from Benin because of a political situation there. He was a qualified accountant but only spoke French and because I was working for a French company, he asked if I could help his relative. My mother agreed for me to help him.

One evening, Mr. Duwa was introduced to me by his cousin. We chatted, and I decided to speak with my manager. I made an appointment with my manager and explained to him that I have a 'cousin' from Benin who speaks French and was looking for an accounting position.

Early next morning as I was getting ready to do school-run and go to work, my three year old daughter came running to me shouting that a barefooted man was looking for me. It was a very desperate looking Mr. Duwa who wanted to find out if there was a job offer. I explained to him that the manager will let me know by next week. Later on, my manager asked me to notify Mr. Duwa to attend an interview on Monday.

On Monday, Mr. Duwa followed me to CFAO for the interview. By Friday he was notified of being successful with the job position as he had managerial experience and spoke French which was helpful.

After a few months, he was promoted to be my manager. I had noticed that his behaviour had changed towards me. He started flirting and harassing me that I should be his girlfriend. Obviously, I refused. I was shocked by his behaviour. He then brought in a young lady called Felicia for me to train as an operator, so she became my assistant. Within three months, the company announced that they need to down-size and there will be redundancies.

Mr. Duwa advised the board members that as I was earning much money they could end my contract and hire an assistant as a cost-cutting measure. And they agreed! I was made redundant. I then found out that my assistant Felicia, who happens to be Mr. Duwa's girlfriend, was promoted to my job.

When my mother found out that I was made redundant, she called Mr. Duwa's cousin and told him what had happened and wondered how someone I helped to get a job could turn around to make me redundant. His cousin apologised to my mother and said he would talk to Mr. Duwa. He later came back to my mother and said Mr. Duwa would try and get me reinstated. Within a few days Mr. Duwa moved out of his cousin's house and was nowhere to be seen again.

I was so sad about losing my job and about what Mr. Duwa had done. I spoke to my

Reverend about the matter. He consoled me and said he will also pray about the situation and asked me to 'leave it with God'. While I was looking for another job, I decided to enroll on a course to study History in the evenings.

Chapter 20

A Dream of Becoming an Air Hostess

One of Mr. E.C. Quaye's daughters, also named Florence was travelling to London to study to become an Air Hostess. When the time came for her to travel, we all gathered at the Airport as a family to see her off. I thought to myself, "what an exciting profession, to be an Air hostess, flying around the world and being able to see places." I became very interested and I told my mother I would like to become an Air hostess. She was silent. Later, she calmly advised me to buy a piece of cloth to be cut into two for both of us to share. She said because I've decided to fly like a bird in the air. It means she will not see me again and that the flying will lead to my death. Therefore, my part of the cloth will be for my burial when I die, and she will use her own piece of the cloth for her own funeral. That was the end of my dream as an Air hostess.

Chapter 21

At the Marketplace

One afternoon, as I was doing the shopping, I heard my name being called from afar. I wondered who could be calling me in this busy market. I then saw a hand gesturing me to come. It turned out to be one of the CFAO's managers, Mr. Boateng. He said he heard of what had happened to me regarding the redundancy. Mr. Boateng said he had been thinking about me all the time because of what he heard. There had been gossip around CFAO of how my relative caused me to lose my job. "My own knife in the cloth has cut me"-a Ghanaian Proverb.

Mr. Boateng said he wanted to help me and that he will speak with the manager in another company called Mr. Morgan, of Ghana Publishing Corporation. He gave me Mr. Morgan's details and asked me to go and see him in a few days for an interview.

After a few days, I got an interview at GPC

with Mr. Morgan and I did the skills test on their machines. I was successful for the position because they had been looking for a machine operator for a while. So I got the job!

Sometimes, I think about how I got this job... imagine in a busy marketplace: jam-packed, lots of noise, a full place and hearing an echo of my name being called from afar in the middle of the market and a hand beckoning me from afar and how it led to my getting a job.

I worked at GPC for approximately three years. There were a lot of changes that took place in my life during this time. One of the changes was that I had decided to separate from Elias because of his unreasonable behaviour towards me when I was unwell and his decision to travel to France without informing me. As we were only engaged, I decided to remove my ring and concentrate on improving my life.

Chapter 22

The Turning Point.

In the same area where I work, there was a salon where I usually got my hair done. I found out that the salon owner also teaches hairdressing so I became interested to learn. I enquired about learning hairdressing and I enrolled on a Sunday course. I would attend after church. There, I got inspired to become a hairdresser. In those days they only did 'press and curl' styles. I became so inspired by hairdressing that I wanted to consider it as a profession. I made up my mind to travel abroad and learn all aspects of hairdressing.

I informed my Manager at GPC of my intention of going to England to learn hairdressing (I chose England because like Ghana, they speak English as opposed to studying in France). I was lucky that he was very supportive of my plans. He then mentioned my plans to our company supplier, Mr. Allen, who worked for an International organisation called McMillan with offices also in London, England. My manager then set up an introductory meeting with myself and Mr. Allen, who mentioned that he would kindly search for hairdressing schools in London for me. A few weeks later, Mr. Allen brought me a prospectus of a school based in Piccadilly Circus called Morris School of Hairdressing. I filled in the prospectus and Mr. Allen kindly sent it for me. Morris School of Hairdressing wrote me with all the details and information regarding the course. I wired the fees required and a letter of confirmation was sent.

I showed the letter of confirmation to my manager and then handed in my notice. The staff at GPC had a going-away party for me and it was even mentioned in our national newspaper that I was going abroad for further studies. My family and friends saw the newspaper article and I also got myself a copy.

My mother was surprisingly happy for me to travel abroad for further studies. She understood my goals to study professional hairdressing abroad and that I will not die in a plane crash. She said that she and the whole family will pray for my safe trip and success on the course. I promised to telephone as soon as I landed in England. So she gave me her blessing to travel.

I planned with Sister Beatrice that Victorine would be living in Togo with her and her numerous half brothers and sisters to continue attending school. My mother would be visiting her and during holidays Victorine will be spending time in Ghana with her. This arrangement will give me the time to concentrate on my course abroad until I return.

Chapter 23

Ashia Cobblah

Travelling Abroad

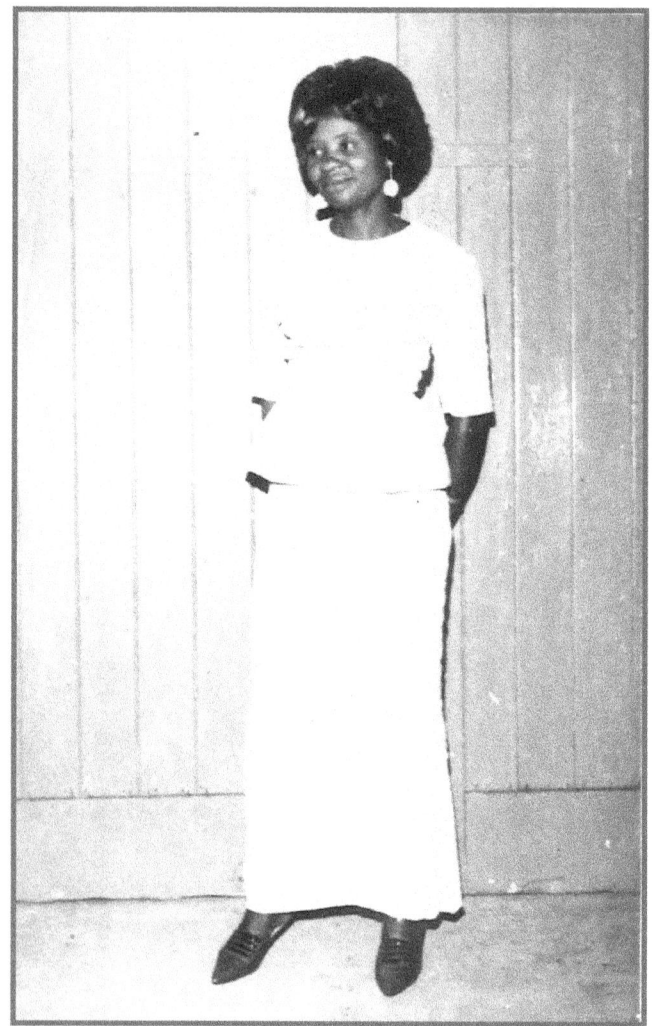

Ashia as a hairdressing student at The Morris School of Hairdressing

I managed to get my travel documents completed and with the help of Mr. Allen, my departure date was confirmed.

Morris School was notified of my date of arrival and a staff was sent to Heathrow airport to meet and escort me to their international students' hostel in North London. As soon as I settled into the hostel, I found the opportunity to call my mother and she wished me the best of luck on the course.

At a local London park, during my culture shock moment, contemplating my future.

I was enrolled on a nine month course, which I commenced in October 1969. Morris was a famous hairdressing school and they were known to train international students. A few months into the course, the school relocated from Piccadilly Circus to large and impressive premises on the Tottenham Court Road.

My student name label of hairdressing textbook

I found the course exciting and to gain more experience, we visited some elderly care homes to practise on their hair, which was helpful.

For the first few weeks, I kept in touch with GPC via Mr. Allen, who was kind enough to visit me at the school a few times to find out how I was because I didn't know anyone in London. I was so grateful for his kindness and I sent greetings to my manager at GPC through him -The kindness of human beings.

At Morris School we only studied on European hair, so I had to find a placement in an Afro hair salon where I could also practise on Afro hair. In London at that time, there were very few Afro Hair Salons.

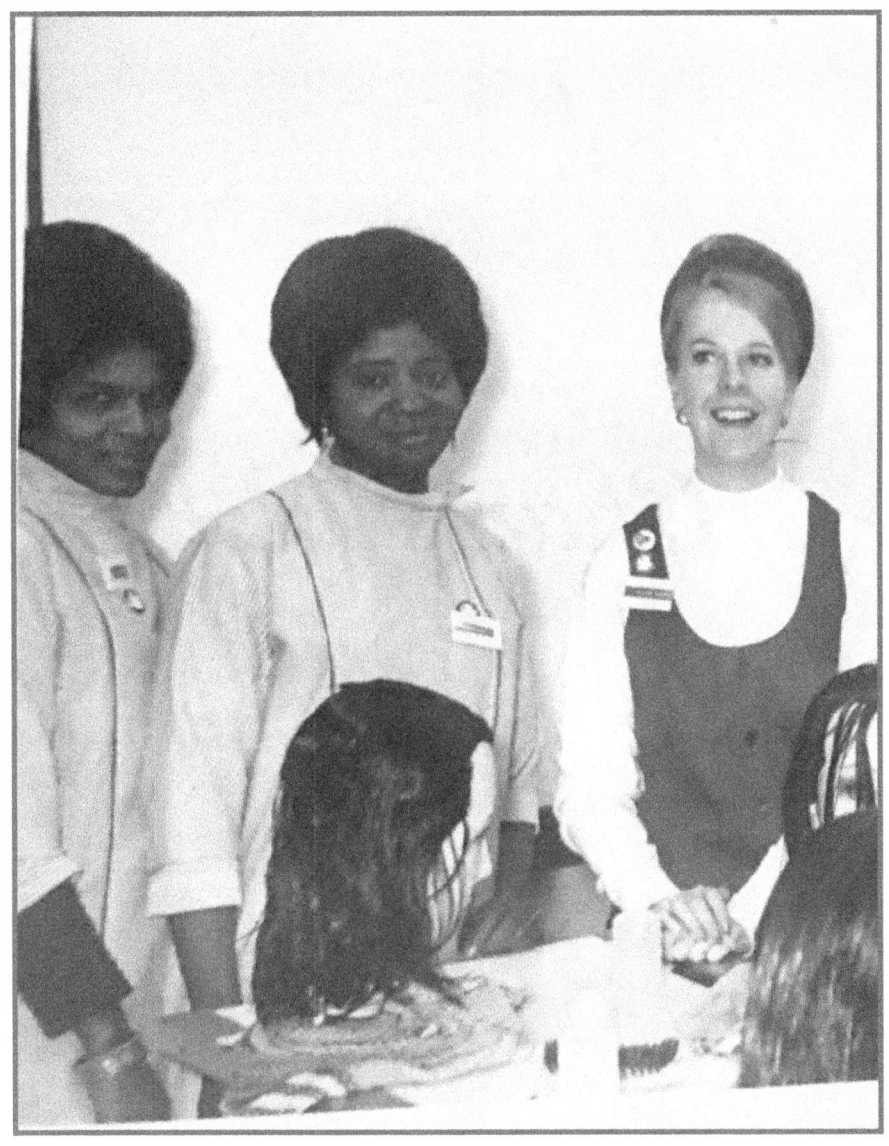

At Morris school, we had studied on European hair only as it was the only hair type available

Chapter 24

Cumberland Hotel

After I graduated, we had to vacate the students' hostel. A school friend, Sue who was also an international student and I decided to find an accommodation together. Luckily through Sue, we found a place at Finsbury Park, at 10 Tollington Road for £2.50-a-week. In those days it was a lot of money. Our house wasn't the best, with one bathroom and two toilets to accommodate all the people living in the four floors. One can only imagine the chaos. So when one of the tenants, a kind Ghanaian lady, Rose was moving to a new property on Old Kent Road, she told me about a vacant property at the Oval. I went to visit the premises at the Oval and it was okay. I quickly moved in and my friend, Sue found a place in Camberwell. After a few months, Sue told me of a more conducive property in Camberwell on Southwell Rd. I informed my landlord and moved to Camberwell.

While I was looking for a placement in an Afro hair salon, I found a Chambermaid job at the Annex of Cumberland Hotel in Marble Arch. After a few weeks, as a chambermaid, I became friendly with the other members of the staff.

They knew I was a qualified hairdresser and some of them allowed me to do their hair (all European hair) and I told them that I was also looking for a hairdressing job in an afro hair salon.

Chapter 25

St. Clair's

A few weeks later, one of my colleagues told me of an afro hair salon around the corner from Cumberland Hotel that I didn't know about. One day, on our day-off, one of my friends took me to the salon to meet the manager. The salon was called St. Clairs', located on Bryanston Street, by the corner from Cumberland Hotel, at Marble Arch. I met Mr. St. Clair and he told me to return the next day to meet his wife, Lorna.

The following day, I went for the appointment to meet Lorna. After the interview, she confirmed that I was accepted on an apprenticeship placement. I gave my notice to end my job as a chambermaid and told my colleagues at the hotel of the good news. We celebrated and I thanked them very much for their help in finding the placement.

My first job at St. Clairs' was as a shampoonist to get familiar with afro hair. I did the role for four months and then progressed to setting, styling and chemical services. As I was on a student visa, the St. Clairs' extended my stay. I was working Mondays to Saturdays, and after a year I was confident and knew how to manage afro hair. In those days in 1971, there were hardly any afro hair salons so we were extremely busy. Sometimes we had no lunch. Some clients usually would have to return the next day as it was hectic. They all couldn't get their hairs done.

My managers, Mr. and Mrs. St. Clair were impressed with the work I was doing and I was promoted to chemical services and a top stylist. I had my own clientele. As a trusted staff at the salon, I was given the salon keys so that the St. Clairs' could go on holiday for the first time in years. They visited their home, the island of St Lucia. I managed the salon for one month and a friend of theirs helped me with the banking.

When the St. Clairs' returned from their holiday, they were impressed and pleased with how the salon was run smoothly and how financially successful it was in their absence. St. Clairs' Salon had become so successful that a second salon was opened at Shepherds' Bush. I was promoted to assistant salon manager at the Marble Arch branch with Mr. St. Clair while Mrs. St. Clair managed the Shepherds' Bush site.

Now that I was stable, I started missing and thinking of Victorine. Both my mother and Beatrice said she was doing fine. I discussed with my mother that I would like her to join me. Within the same time, I got a message that Elias had died. I spoke with Mr. & Mrs. St. Clair about the death of Victorine's father and asked if I could go to Ghana to see my family. I also told them that I would be bringing my daughter, Victorine, back with me. I went for a month and came back to London with Victorine. I enrolled her in the local primary school and arranged for my neighbour to do the school run.

Chapter 26

A Turning Point

As helpful as I am, a Ghanaian man who I knew, had asked me if I could find a salon placement at St. Clairs' for his wife, as she was desperately looking for an internship after graduating from a training school.

I mentioned it to Mrs St. Clair that a 'relative' of mine was looking for a placement, so she agreed that Janet can join us.

Within a month of her joining, I realised she had become closer with the other staff members and started gossiping.

They in-turn became unfriendly towards me.

What was disappointing was that Janet became jealous and malicious towards me, the person who I had found the placement for!

I went and mentioned the problem to Janet's husband and the next day, she came to the salon and told the other staff that her husband was upset with her because of my complaint. The salon environment became hostile and it became challenging for me to work with the other members of staff as we were no longer working as a team. After a few months, I mentioned the difficulties to Mr. St. Clair. He reminded me that she was my 'relative' and there was not much he could do except to tell all the staff to work as a team. The salon atmosphere did not change, it was still hostile. It became unbearable for me, so I decided to leave. I was sad as I did not want to leave St Clairs'. I loved working with them.

On a Monday morning, the opportunity came when I arrived late to work. There was huge traffic around the West End which was caused by a bomb disposal operation at Selfridges. Mr. St. Clair was busy when I finally got to the salon. I apologised for being late and gave the reason. I then quietly mentioned to him that I am resigning and I left the salon keys in the office. He was surprised and adamant but because he was busy, there was not much he could do.

Chapter 27

Home Salon Days

One of my school friends had found a much better property at Camberwell, so I rented a place there. After a few days, of contemplating, I informed my friends and neighbours that I am now doing hair in my house. I designated a few days of the week to do hair by appointment. My friends were beneficiaries and they told their friends of my 'home-salon'. 'Word of mouth' was productive and successful. I was busy most days. I had time to ponder and plan my future in hairdressing.

Surprisingly, I noticed that there were a lot of Africans and Caribbeans in London and I wondered why there were hardly any African-Caribbean businesses. I didn't understand why. This was an opportunity to have a business to provide hair services for the community. After a few months and with the encouragement of my friends, I decided to look for a small shop so that I could open my own salon.

Chapter 28

Looking for premises.

I started collecting brochures and leaflets about salon business from salon design companies and planned on how to open a small salon. I was living in Camberwell at this time and I used to do my shopping in Brixton because it was the place where tropical foods were sold. I noticed a lot of African and Caribbean people were also doing shopping there. But there was no prominent salon in the Lambeth area except for a very tiny salon run by Mr. Cole on Atlantic road. He was a friendly and jovial fellow who only opened for business when he felt like. I also observed that it was only Mr. Martin in Granville Arcade selling afro hair and cosmetics and also a West Indian bakery. Some days, I used to walk around Brixton and the surrounding areas looking for a salon property. There were only a few salons for European hair.

Chapter 29

Brixton Underground

In 1971, the Brixton underground was opened. It was connecting to the Victoria line. There were some shops available in the arcade. There was an Italian coffee shop situated in front of the arcade. I went in and enquired about the availability of vacant shops. The coffee shop owners were George and his wife. George advised me to go to the underground information office to enquire. Luckily, there were a few shops in the arcade that were still vacant because Brixton at that time was labelled a 'no-go' area. Some people were hesitant to go there because apparently Brixton was labelled a 'high-crime' area. However, I have never encountered or witnessed any crime, so I was a bit confused by this labelling of Brixton. Even taxis did not want to drive to Brixton as it was 'south of the river'.

The underground information officer advised me to contact their headquarters at Victoria near the Army & Navy Store. At the meeting, at the London Underground headquarters, they asked me what type of business I would be doing, and we discussed the details of what is involved in the business. I was asked to return in two weeks for them to have time to find out whether the business would be suitable in the arcade.

I returned two weeks later for further meeting and discussion. After an hour-long session, they said they will 'put a letter in the post' as regards to their decision. A few weeks later, I received a welcome letter. They had agreed for me to open a salon in the arcade. Within a week, I went to the Brixton Underground to collect the keys. I was now going to become an owner of a hairdressing salon in Brixton. It was such an overwhelming feeling.

From The Gold Coast To Electric Avenue

Newly opened Brixton Underground station

With the letter and my business plan, I went to the National Westminster Bank on Brixton High Street, to make an appointment for a business loan. The manager was very helpful and accommodating. The bank manager was pleased that I wanted to open a business in Brixton because the area was quiet and needed regeneration.

Chapter 30

Ashia Hairdressing Salon at 8 Station Arcade, Brixton

A junior member of staff outside the salon

After picking up the keys, it became essential to beat the time because my goal was to open the salon within a month. I contacted all necessary companies to work on the empty shop to make it into my desired salon: from the salon fixtures and fittings, designs, signboards and product deliveries. I managed to get everything on credit.

As for the naming of the salon, it was essential for me to name it "Ashia" and not Florence, simply because no-one knew me as Ashia, but as Florence. For the sake of the St. Clairs' and their salon, I didn't want them to lose any of their clients. I knew that the clients I had built-up in their salon may naturally be looking for where I was. But it was essential for me not to take any of their clients. I was aware that it was a common practice for hairdressers to pull their clientele when leaving their workplace to set-up their own business. But that was not my practice. It was necessary for me not to 'steal' St. Clairs' clients. I detest that behaviour and action. I suppose, as a believer and a Christian, it was necessary for me and it naturally played a part in my standing on this issue. I stand by the famous Proverbs… "Do unto others as you would want them do unto you".

The St. Clairs' were good people and they were my 'first family' in London and I will always respect them for teaching me how to do Afro hair. I believe I needed to generate my own clientele that was why I named the salon 'Ashia.'

<u>A few of my staff from both Caribbean and African backgrounds at 8 Brixton Station Arcade.</u>

Chapter 31

Grand Opening of Ashia Hairdressing Salon in 1976

I had already prepared the entire plan of the salon fixtures & fittings in advance. I immediately contacted the salon designers to design the interior and the signboard for the exterior. I gave the designers four days (Monday to Thursday) to complete the fittings, while I was preparing the leaflets and posters to promote the grand opening. I was also interviewing and hiring staff. I hired three stylists to commence the business. By Friday everything was in place for the grand opening. The ceremony was grand indeed and I was amazed at the turnout.

As the business began, I was pleased with the rapid growth. I was able to pay the staff. We hired juniors to assist the stylist so we were working effortlessly and professionally. After a few weeks, we had settled the day-to-day operation of running the salon. Our leading product suppliers were the charming team of gentlemen: Mr. Lincoln (Len) Dyke, Mr. Dudley Dryden, both from Jamaica.

**Dyke & Dryden Ltd. The Hair and Beauty Wholesaler/Distributor
(image from their book cover)**

The Dyke & Dryden business was created in 1965 as music distributors and sellers located in Tottenham, North London. In 1968, Mr. Tony Wade, from Montserrat joined the team to create Britain's largest Black-owned company of hair and beauty distributors as well as wholesalers. They were friendly and down-to-earth, great to do business with and they genuinely cared about their customers and well-being. This pioneering empire became Britain's first black multi-million-pound business enterprise, deservingly.

We also used to support and buy products from Me Amigo, another Caribbean-owned product distributor and wholesaler.

These were some of the notable events:

Miss Teenager of The West Indies in Great Britain Beauty Pageant Winner. The photographers came with her, so we were published in the South London Press newspaper and other publications.

Miss Teenager of The West Indies in Great Britain Beauty Pageant Winner 1978

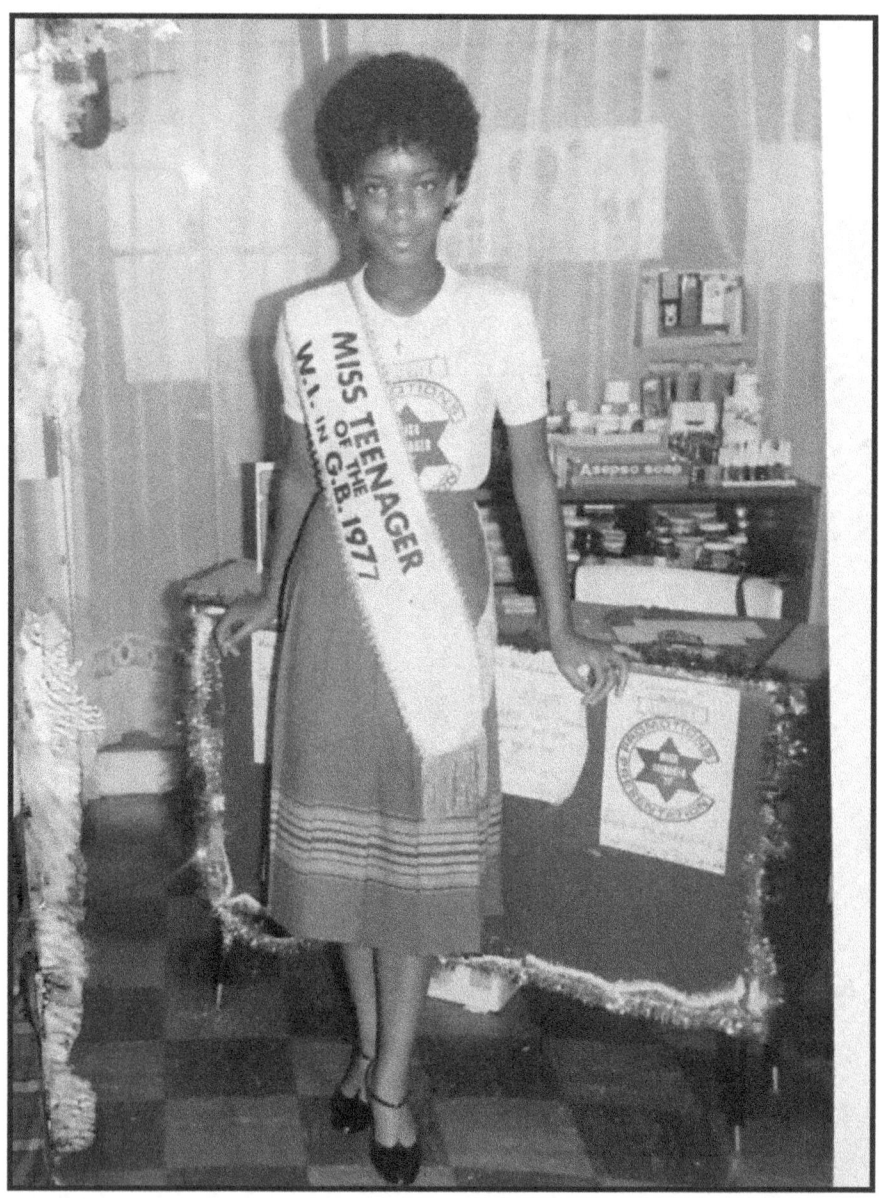

Miss Teenager of The West Indies in Great Britain Beauty Pageant Winner 1977

Miss Teenager of The West Indies Beauty in GB winners in 1970s were provided with complimentary hairstyles by my salon, two years running.

A company came from Chicago, the U.S., to introduce **Nail Extension** service to the U.K., an essential American trend and sculptured nails and nail extensions. The company trained my daughter and some of my staff to open a nail section in the salon. After several weeks, we decided not to continue with the nail extension service as we found it to weaken and damage the natural nails. I believe we were one of the first afro hair salons in London to introduce the nail art and extensions.

In-Salon Seminars

We had several invitations from African American hair care companies to introduce their latest line of products in England: Soft Sheen's Care Free Curl, Bronner Brothers and Ellante Vitale.

Bronner Brothers

I had a very close relationship with the Bronner Brothers family. It started with using their products. The company began in 1947 by Dr. Nathaniel H. Bronner Sr., his brother Arthur Sr. and their sister Emma Bronner. They had become one of the largest and most successful African American hair & skin care companies in the world. They were known for their annual BB International beauty and trade shows in Atlanta- a convention that has become the country's largest African-American beauty show. A representative would visit my salon to acquaint with me as I was one of their biggest users in the U.K. I had a very close relationship with the Bronner Brothers family. It started with using their products. The company began in 1947 by Dr. Nathaniel H. Bronner Sr., his brother Arthur Sr. and their sister Emma Bronner.

They had become one of the largest and most successful African American hair & skin care companies in the world. They were known for their annual BB International beauty and trade shows in Atlanta- a convention that has become the country's largest African-American beauty show. A representative would visit my salon to acquaint with me as I was one of their biggest users in the U.K.

The Bronner Family Photo.

I was invited to Atlanta to the hair convention in the 1980s. One of my assistants and I went for a few days. The family asked me to their house and they laid out dinner in my honour for supporting them in business. The dinner table was one of the largest tables I have ever dined on. It was a joyous occasion. The beauty show was one of the most exciting and of great magnitude. Americans are known for their grand exhibitions. It was incredibly exciting. They also invited me to one of their son's wedding two weeks later but I was too busy to attend.

AHBAI

Their brand was a member of the American Health and Beauty Aids Institute founded in 1981: an internationally renowned business membership association representing the world's leading African-American owned companies that manufacture hair and beauty related products.

The AHBAI "The Proud Lady" symbol was to signify that it was produced and owned by black businesses and in turn to re-invest in the African-American community. The symbol was found on the back of all African-American hair and beauty products.

UK Hairdressing Membership Affiliation

Our salon was a member of HABIA-Hair & Beauty Industry Authority and C.A.S.H.-Caribbean & Afro Society of Hairdressers. I was a State Registered Hairdresser recognised by the hairdressing council, a statutory body set up by Parliament.

The Spending Power of African-Caribbean Community Research confirmed that the spending power of Britain's black community was estimated at over £300 billion. I had not thought of how lucrative our beauty industry was as it turns out it was worth billions! In the early 1980s in Brixton, I noticed Indians began to open afro hair and beauty shops. The same expansions began in Peckham.

Chapter 32

VIP Clientele

<u>With MP Lord Paul Boateng and Mrs. Boateng at a function</u>

We styled hair for the wife of the MP and now Lord Paul Boateng for their wedding. Her mother was also a regular customer. When we moved to the larger salon, Victorine was Mr. Boateng's personal barber for some time. There were few other TV personalities and entertainers who had also visited my salon.

A photo with Azumah Nelson at a function

I attended a West African gathering, photo taken with Former president & former Head of state Yakubu Gowan

Caribbean Cultural Function at the Porchester

I do not recall the name of this event which was organised by the Caribbean community and was annually held at the Porchester. Our salon was the only ticket-seller in Brixton for the annual dinner & dance event because one of my Caribbean staff suggested that we sell the tickets of the game also because of the popularity of the salon with the Caribbean clients.

It was such a popular event that when it was close to the time of the game, I was swamped with selling tickets and taking calls to reserve tickets. It was a high-demand event. I remembered that some people will call from Birmingham to save the cards as it was sold out in their area.

The Porchester was located at Bayswater and was usually crowded on Saturday nights. I always received invitations from the organisers of Caribbean Cultural Event. But because it was held on Saturdays, the busiest salon-day, it was not possible to attend. Most Saturdays we worked until past 10 p.m. I managed to attend one year, and it was an exciting event. I got to know why it was such a popular event.

A Salon business partnership in France

A French woman named Georgina visited my salon and requested a meeting with me. She wanted to propose a business in France, Le Havre where she based.

After a few meetings and I got to know her, I decided to become her business partner.

After Victorine and I visited Georgina in Le Havre, we opened a beauty salon in France. To promote the business, we put on a hair and fashion show by taking along about 15 young models from the U.K. The company operated for 5 years.

Chapter 33

Helping my family members

I invited two of my sisters and two nieces to learn hairdressing. I trained my two sisters in the salon. Although I was swamped, I was wondering how I could be a benefit to my home country of Ghana. I was contemplating if it was possible to open a salon because I was too busy to return to Ghana at the time. There was political unrest and the country was unstable.

I then discussed with my sisters, Felicia and Paulina to know who could manage a salon in Accra, Ghana. We decided that my niece Cecelia, 'Baby' (as we affectionately call her) would be suitable. I found her a prestigious hairdressing school in the West End of London. Cecelia attended and graduated with a Diploma in International hairdressing.

I also trained my other niece, Aku in the salon. By then my sisters were fully trained and had returned to Ghana to start their businesses.

I managed to help them set up their own businesses in Ghana by sending equipment and products.

Chapter 34

'A Need for a Bigger/Larger Salon'

Within two years, I realised the salon at station arcade was too small. We needed a more prominent Salon. I was also considering having a school. Apart from training my sisters and a few of my stylists, I was also receiving enquiries from people wanting to learn afro hairdressing. We also realised that there were no prominent afro hair schools in England.

I then sent my daughter, Victorine to the reputable Pivot Point International and Research Centre for Cosmetology and Bio-Aesthetics in Chicago in the United States, to learn the arts of hair and beauty for her to eventually run the hairdressing school when she returns. I suppose this would make up for the time she had earlier refused to attend a private school in Oxford years ago.

We had a medium-sized business with four

styling stations. It got to the point where clients were being turned away. We were losing a lot of clients because of the limited size of our salon. Some days, clients will be waiting at the door before we open for business. We were getting desperate with the situation.

There were a few Ugandan Indians who came to me for advice on where they could get business shop. These Indians were business owners who were expelled from Uganda by President Idi Amin.

Chapter 35

Ashia Cobblah

Getting Married

My Wedding Day at St Georges Cathedral, London 2nd April 1977

My friends were worried about me and kept making comments that I lived for the business. Though I would be tired after busy Saturdays, I sometimes made efforts to attend weddings, christenings or funeral functions.

There was a Sierra Leonean neighbour who lived close by when I was living in Camberwell. She introduced herself as Adeiza and was friendly to me. One day she asked me where I was from and whether I was married. I demanded to know why she was asking. She said she had noticed that I was not wearing a wedding ring and she wanted to introduce me to one of her relatives who was nice and single.

Within a few days, this lady came to my door with a man. My daughter opened the door for them because I was asleep. Victorine came to wake me up and told me that I had visitors. I was surprised with this visit because I had not given her my address. She explained that she was knocking on all the doors on my road before she reached No.98 and that she recognised my daughter. I welcomed them, but I was irritated because my sleep was disturbed. Adeiza introduced her relative called Mr. Koroma. I was polite and made the visit short so I could go back to sleep.

A few days later Mr. Koroma came to visit by himself but I told him that I was not interested but he was persistent. I realised how calm and polite he was. He was good at discussions. We used to discuss many issues.

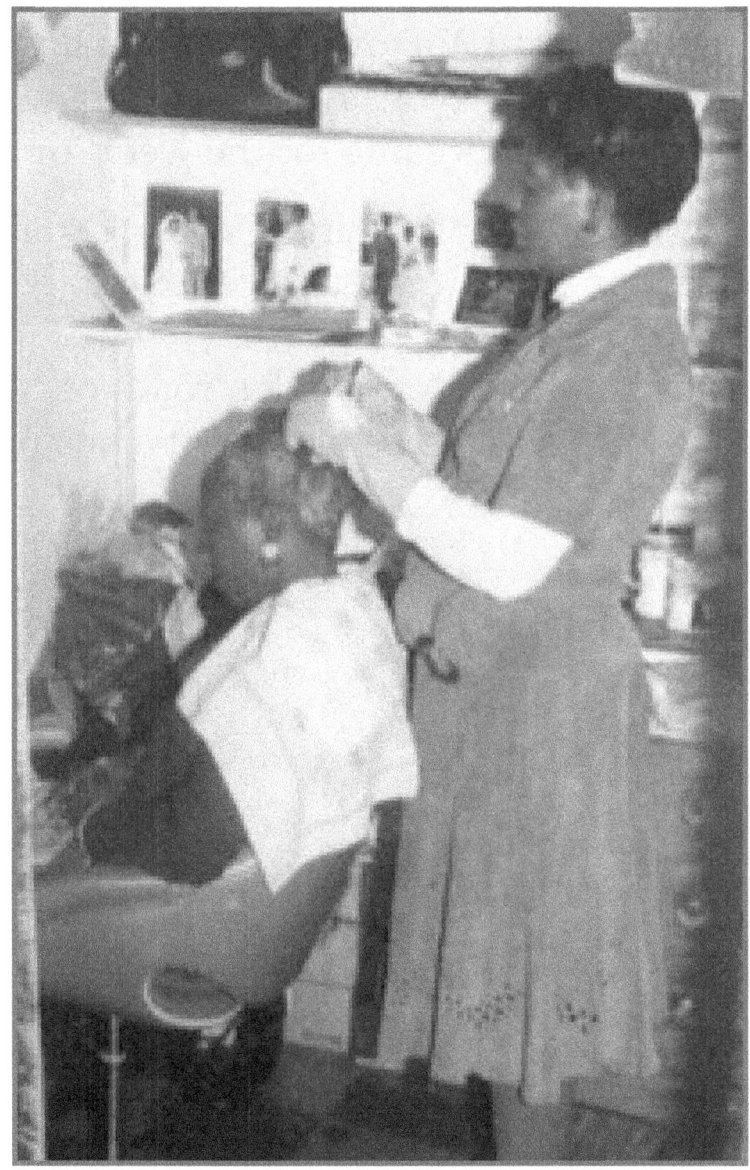

Ashia at 8 stations Arcade, after honeymoon doing a client's hair treatment

Sometimes, I would come home and he would be cooking with Victorine. I eventually got married to him. It was a lavish affair. My mother and sisters came for the wedding.

We were now living in a council flat in Kennington from where we managed to save a deposit to buy a house. We eventually purchased a house on Porden road, off Acre Lane in 1979 so as to be close to the business.

Chapter 36

Ashia Cobblah

New Bigger Salon on Electric Avenue

Sometime in the 1980s, we were in desperate need of a more prominent salon in the same area. When I was not busy in the salon, I would take a walk around Brixton to look for an empty shop to rent. One of the days, I came across a suitable site, an empty jewellery shop on Electric Avenue. The historic street is known for being the first to have electricity in the whole of London. I telephoned the estate agent in charge of the Lambeth businesses. I gave all my details and my interest in the property.

On one of the days, I came across a suitable site, an empty jewellery shop on Electric Avenue. The historic street is known for being the first to have electricity in the whole of London.

I telephoned the estate agent in charge of the Lambeth businesses. I gave all my details and my interest in the property.

Iconic sign for the famous Electric Avenue, Present Day.

The property consisted of 3 floors: The ground-floor alone measured over 1,280 square feet, the first floor and basement. I planned to have the salon on the ground floor because it was spacious. I considered using the first floor as an education centre and the basement for wholesale business.

However, my major concern with the site was that it had gutters and I needed to spend a lot of money to refurbish the building and redesign it into a viable salon. After a few days of negotiation, within a few weeks, I received the legal papers to 11 Electric Avenue. I agreed to accept the property and I signed the necessary legal papers.

My plan was for us to relocate to this new site within 3 months which we managed to do. We were able to relocate and transfer the business to Electric Avenue on time to prepare for the grand opening.

Chapter 37

Grand Opening of Ashia Hair design Ltd (on Electric Ave.)

It was a lavish affair. The Lambeth Business Alliance, the Council and my National Westminster Bank manager were all in attendance for the grand opening. The newspapers and photographers were invited to document the whole affair. The salon on the ground floor had over 25 stations and areas which comprised of 12 styling stations, 4 chemical service areas, 4 shampoo & treatment areas, 4 braiding areas, a management office and a large reception and a waiting area.

The salon was well sophisticated and large to accommodate the number of clients at the busiest time. This was usually seen at the weekends when most of the customers come for their hair do. At some stage, we had to employ over 25 staff who worked until past 8pm.

Standing outside Electric Avenue Salon

I believe it was one of the most prominent salons in Lambeth if not in London. It measured over 1,280+ square feet.

ASHIA HAIR DESIGN SALON: *This view of the salon shows the extensive range of professional equipment available to the students during their salon experience*

Front of Salon interior

Sitting in my office desk, taking care of the business side of the salon

Ashia at reception and retail area of the shop at Electric Avenue

Ashia at the new retail section for hair extensions and weaves

The launch of hair products

As numerous amounts of hair products were required for afro hair, two products were popular with afro hair at the time. So I contacted my chemist friend to create a hair moisturising cream and scalp oil which became very popular.

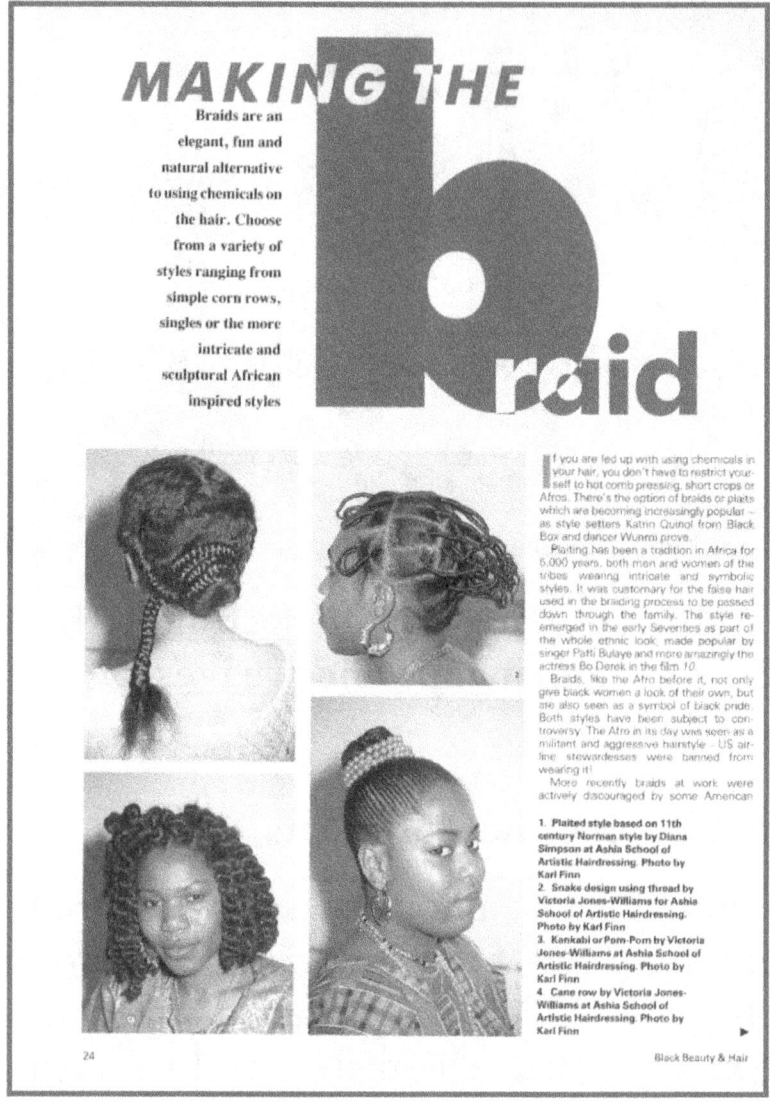

The Kankabi Feature Hair Magazine

Our salon introduced The Kankabi to the UK.

In those days in London, there were chemically processed hairstyles for women. There were no authentic African hairstyles for afro hair. One of my stylists returned from holiday in Ghana and suggested if we could introduce new hairstyles that were popular in Ghana and across Africa. Our salon introduced beautiful plaiting styles and Corkscrew hairstyle known as 'The Kankabi.' It became a trendy hairstyle across London and parts of England for several years.

<u>Ashia advising and consulting a client while her sister, Paulina was training at the desk</u>

Busy salon event day 1990

Publication Features

<u>Ashia feature in local Newspapers: The Voice & South London Press.</u>

Ashia featured in Hair & Beauty Magazines: Hairdressers' Journal and Black Beauty & Hair

An Award-Winning Salon

One of the humbling but amazing highlights was, Ashia Hair Design Salon winning the first-ever national Afro Hairstyling competition in 1983, created by Dyke & Dryden Ltd. It was a triumphant win. It was evidence of our hard work being recognised and acknowledged.

<u>Ashia wins the 1st. ever national Afro Hair styling competition</u>

From The Gold Coast To Electric Avenue

<u>Our Customer's Loyalty Christmas gifts</u>

Christmas cards, I was the model on the cards

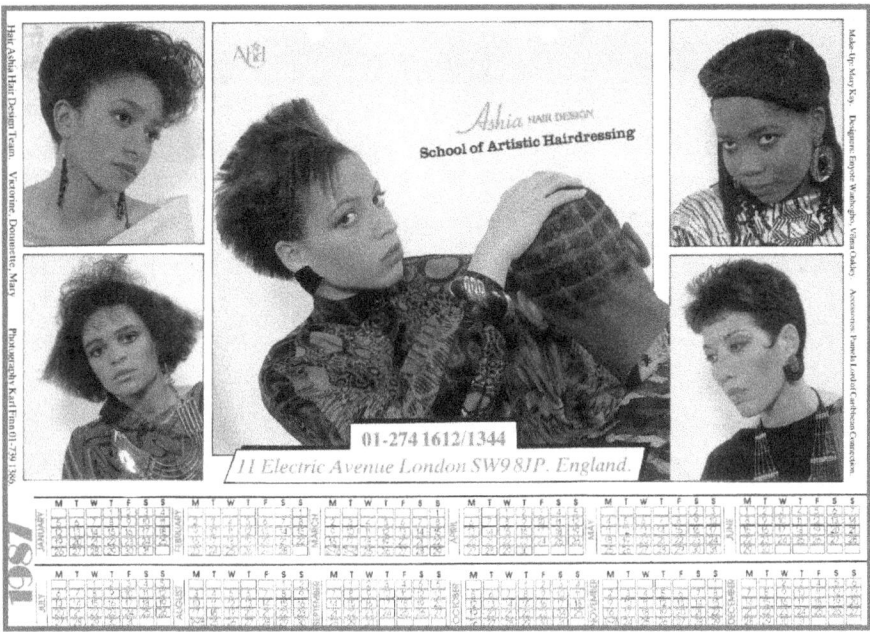

Our client's Salon Calendar gift

Salon Pensioners Day

Introduction of Hair service for the Elderly

Wednesdays were dedicated to my elderly clients. I devised a pensioners' day to have their hair done for £1. It became very popular. It was good to be doing something great for the community, especially for the elderly.

Chapter 38

Opening Panache Hair salon in Ghana

Panache salon

After graduating from a prestigious International hairdressing school, my niece 'Baby' returned to Ghana to open The Panache Salon. It was a large salon and was not far from The Kwame Nkrumah Circle in the heart of the city of Accra. A lot of tourists from abroad also used to get their hair done there.

Her VIP clients were President J.J. Rawlings and the First Lady of Ghana as well as other celebrities. It was also a central place for American hair beauty companies to launch their products. The salon became very well-known across Ghana and was popular with Television and radio broadcasters. Eventually, five of my family members became hairdressers. My sister Paulina opened a salon in Tema and one of my nephews opened a salon in Benin.

Chapter 39

Making an impact without realising

I didn't realise how I had become a role model for a lot of women to open their own salons across England, Europe and parts of Africa. I indeed did not realise the impact I've made in the lives of a lot of people except for some people's comments which made me to become aware.

A visit from Norman

One day a young man of Caribbean origin came to the salon and he asked to speak with me. The receptionist notified me of a visitor. He introduced himself and requested if he could talk with me for a few minutes. As I was not busy that day, I agreed and took him to my office for a talk. As soon as we got in the office, he did something astonishing. He suddenly hugged me and started crying saying that I made him who he had become by inspiring him and other people.

At that moment I realised there were lack of role models and opportunities. He said that he had observed how I had opened the first salon and how well the business was doing and that it gave him an idea to attend hairdressing school.

Norman further explained that I was his role model and for a lot of people in Brixton, Lambeth and beyond, to make them consider going into business. He went further to say, although a lot of them haven't come forward to tell me, he is proud to come to let me know especially because he was doing very well in his business, with two salons: one in Stockwell and another on Walworth Road.

He invited me to visit his salon at Stockwell, and I made time to visit. I was very happy for him. I recall him mention, *"If Ashia can do it, so can we."*

A lady in Streatham.

I met a lady in a Streatham salon and when she realised I was Ashia, she was shocked. She then explained: *"It was because of you, my mother who was studying Law decided to change to hairdressing."*

Beauty and looks

A hair-raising experience —
psychedelic hair care and grooming

A lot of people are now giving more attention to their hair than ever. Our grooming expert, Jane Buma-Francis, has been finding out . . .

Hair care for women is not a novelty. Women have always paid attention to their hair, but what is new is the considerable amount of money and time being devoted to this. Recent research conducted by Berteo Group Ltd; shows that most females of working age and above spend about a quarter of their incomes and a third of their non-working hours on their hair, and that 60% of the females interviewed would rather forgo a meal than see their hair unattended to!! But females are not alone in this. Men are equally taking care of their hair in a countless variety of styles, treatment and grooming that range from mod to mad. Thus one is not surprised these days to find men toning, dyeing, curling or changing their hair's natural texture in an attempt to look more trendy.

Why then this all-consuming hair care bug? Mrs. Koroma, proprietress of the ever-busy Ashia Hair Salon and School of Hairdressing in London S.W.9 explained that social acceptability, the need to look cute and show off have a dominating influence on the way people take care of themselves, particularly that most conspicuous part of the human body, the hair. She added that younger people like to show that they are 'with it' while 'senior citizens' want to prove that they are still 'in circulation'.

It is appreciated and socially accepted to look cute, if one is to fit into today's society, more so when many occupations nowadays demand personal attention. The wide range of cosmetics, conditioners, shampoos and oils that now overflow in the hair and beauty market aided by the professional and creative hands of some salons such as St. Clairs of Shepherds Bush, W12; Ashia Salon of Brixton S.W.9; Holywood Curls of Kilburn N.W.6, Bab-zee's of West Green Road, N.15; Soul Scissors of Catford S.E.6; Aquarius Hair Fashions of Finsbury Park, N.4; Chez Lucie of Maida Vale, W.9; Baron of Knightsbridge, W.13; C. Wett Hair & Beauty Salon of Uxbridge Road, W.12; Collette Salon of Clapham, S.W.4; Afro Glamourland of Dalston, E.8; Supreme Design of Turnpike Lane, N.8 and some others (where clients not only enjoy comfortable atmosphere, attentive service and advice on styles that fit individual facial structures, but also offer other services such as pedicare, manicure, electrolysis, steam and wax bath, toning and massage) all of which have added immensely to a greater appreciation of psychedelic hair care and grooming. •

From The Gold Coast To Electric Avenue

In the limelight

Ashia Salon & School of Hairdressing

IF you think you have not heard of Ashia Salon then jog your memory, for that day when your hair was done in SW London and every piece of it was perfectly in its place and you were the cynosure of all eyes, you most probably have just stepped out of Ashia Salon.

It will be emphasizing the obvious to traditional Londoners to introduce Ashia Salon but for tourists and people who are newly settled in London, suffice it to say that this salon symbolizes the very epitome of anisex hair care; whether African, European, Caribbean or Asian. The 'Ashia Empire' as it is fondly known by numerous satisfied clients, occupies three large floors in 11 Electric Avenue in Brixton, London S.W.9. The Sales Department, a very busy place where all kinds of hair products are sold, is in the lower ground. The hair-dressing salon occupies the ground floor and is a kaleidoscopic rendezvous for the smart and sophisticated set. The spotless reception area with its relaxed atmosphere, the prompt service and attentiveness of the professional stylists have all contributed to the edge which the salon has over many others.

The proprietress Mrs Florence Koroma, however, has other reasons for the success of the salon. 'Apart from the fact that we have highly qualified, experienced and dedicated stylists, we study clients' facial structures and decide with them on the best styles putting into consideration their ability to manage those styles,' Mrs Koroma says. She should know. She trained in hair-dressing and beauty care and has fifteen years post qualification experience making people look stunningly beautiful.

On the first floor is the Ashia School of Hairdressing — a recognised institute run by Mrs Koroma's very pleasant daughter, Victorine. A licensed cosmetologist trained in U.S.A., Victorine is a stylist, instructor and hair-care expert combined. The school was launched by both women in 1982 and it runs a highly intensive nine months course in all aspects of hair-care and beauty including laying out a salon and methods of examining hair products for their chemical contents. Her students are drawn from many countries, many of whom have passed out and have established flourishing salons elsewhere. Tuition fee for the course is £1,400.00 including V.A.T. and £400.00 worth of equipment. Victorine enjoys the challenges of her profession but says that a very time-consuming aspect of it is putting her fingers on the tap for new products 'for purposes of examining and ascertaining their usefulness. This entails very wide reading of relevant materials and being in constant touch with hair-product manufacturers. I really have to nose around and keep my eyes and ears open.'

The Koromas' interest in research and enterprise have added new discoveries in hair and skin care technology. Among the products they now use and market are the natural silky hair tonic and oil which can be absorbed through scalp cells and help in the prevention of dandruff and itching. They also use ballet silky cream made from the fibroin extracted from natural pure silk. This fine and white cream is indispensable for ladies and gentlemen of all ages who want to keep their skin smooth and soft. Unlike some other products, they have no side effects. Also used in pearl cream which is effective in improving the nutritional conditions of the skin, keeping the balance of secretion of fat and water, promoting action of the cells and moistening the skin. Mrs Koroma is full of praise for these new products. 'The pearl cream substances are produced in the Taihu Lake, Jiangsu, China and rank first in the country in quality. The minerals and organic substances they contain have high nutritive value and pharmaceutical effects. They are invaluable raw material for anti-decrepitude and skin-care cosmetics. We are lucky to discover these new products which we have examined and found very useful. We stock them and our clients are very happy with them.'

Services in the salon include braiding, hair colouring, cut and blow dry, hair relaxing, permanent wave (curls), conditioning, treatment and hair designing. Both school and salon enjoy high patronage and that is because the quality of services rendered is excellent. •

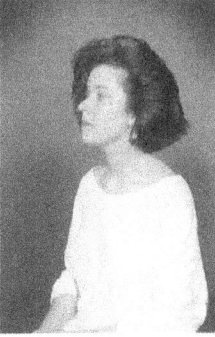

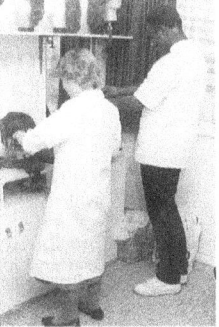

The students are practising on slip-ons for experience and demonstration before being allowed to work on live models or clients.

The Two Newspapers that Ashia Salon was featured in

Ashia Cobblah

The two major Hair and Beauty Magazines Ashia Salon was featured in.

Chapter 40

Ashia Cobblah

Memorable Events

The beauty of Africa Event at Hammersmith Town Hall

Actual Front cover Of Event Program

From The Gold Coast To Electric Avenue

A lavish event was held at the iconic Town Hall. A full evening program from 8p.m. till <u>2 a.m.</u>

<u>A message from Lord Pitt of Hampstead</u>

This event is one of my proudest moments, it was a program dedicated to raising funds for Britain's first multi-cultural Residential Centre at Polebrook House.

The theme was: *'The Beauty of Africa: Past and present'*. We had a line-up of talented dancers and performers. The magnificent event was organized by our public relations personnel, Jane Hammond. All the proceeds from the evening were dedicated to the centre.

Every year in the summer, I used to hold a 'Traditional Wear and Dance competition' at The Clapham Common Hall. An exciting raffle draw would be held for guests to win prizes of beauty products for the first, second and third winners. The event was for Africans and non-Africans. It was a fun, educational and exciting event.

PROGRAMME

8.00 pm	Ashia stylists and students welcome you with a glass of Ashia Punch
8.30 pm	Mrs Florence Koroma of Ashia Salon & School introduces comperes Nana Esso (Akan-speaking) and Dorothy Ottey (English-speaking)
9.00 pm	Buffet opens — see menu on next page
9.15 pm	Stella Starr sings South African solo and the Ashia Singers perform Welcome Song
9.30 pm	Miss Victorine Koroma of Ashia School introduces

THE BEAUTY OF AFRICA — PAST AND PRESENT

ACT 1: THE PAST

Scene 1

Tutankhamun's Treasurer Maya and his wife arise from their newly-discovered tomb in Egypt's Valley of the Kings to bring you the fashions of 1300 BC

Scene 2

The Adzido Dancers, hair braided in styles fashionable for time out of mind, bring you a drama from an Ewe village in West Africa

Scene 3

The Akwaaba Dancers, dressed in the kente cloth as worn at the court of the nineteenth-century Ashanti monarch, King Osei Bonsu, perform a dance fit for royalty

10.00 pm	**INTERVAL**
	Dr Aaron Haynes, Clerk to the Trustees, Community Roots Trust, presents the case for Polebrook
10.15 pm	**INTERLUDE**
	Snaky Joe performs the Voodoo Snake Dance with his two 13-foot pythons and 17-foot boa constrictor
10.30 pm	**ACT II: THE PRESENT**

The following five designers bring you the beauty of today's fashions, all influenced by their roots in Africa's past:

YOMI KHAN: Jamaican-born, she shows outfits made in hessian and using bold colours, reflecting a rural influence.

FADDIS: This African/European duo draws on the cultural roots of both partners with a collection of casual outfits, including bush jackets and safari suits in traditional patterns, right out of Africa

DAPHNE SALOMON: Her batik and tye dyed cottons are designed and made in her native Sierra Leone to traditional and contemporary designs

SHELLEYS DESIGNS: Jamaican-born Co-Ordinator for the whole fashion show, Shelley Crawford features African-style eveningwear with matching hats

ENYOTE WANHOGO: Nigerian-born, she shows the printed silk scarves and fabrics for which she is becoming well-known at many stores, including Liberty's of Regent Street

11.15 pm	Dancing to Flamingo Sounds Disco
12.00	Buffet closes
	Dancing to Native Spirit High Life Band, led by Herman Asafo (bassist) Guest Singers: Pat Thomas and Henrietta Alele
12.30 am	Adzido Dancers perform traditional South and West African dances
1.00 am	Raffle is drawn
1.15 am	Dancing continues to Native Spirit High Life Band
1.50 am	Ghanaian Farewell Song
2.00 am	Akwaaba Evening ends

Programme for the Akwaaba Evening

MENU
(All prices listed are per portion or cup)

Jolloff Rice (recipe includes chicken)	£2.00	Mango	75p
Fried Chicken	£1.00	Jamaican Patties	£1.00
Fried Fish	£1.00	Salad	75p
Boiled Rice	50p	Hot Dogs	75p
Curried Goat	£1.00	Coffee	30p
Kelewele (cubed fried plantain)	50p	Tea	25p

RAFFLE
During the Akwaaba Evening, tickets will be sold for a raffle in aid of Community Roots Trust, to be drawn at 1.00 am

PEOPLE BEHIND THE SCENES
The Hosts

Hosts for the Akwaabba Evening are Mrs Florence Ashia Koroma and her daughter, Victorine. Mrs Koroma this year celebrates her tenth anniversary as proprietor of Ashia Hair Design Salon in Brixton and her fourth as Principal of Ashia School of Artistic Hairdressing, of which Miss Koroma is Course Director.

In its first year one of the Ashia School's students, Essie Annan from Ghana, won the Afro Hair & Beauty '83 Styling Trophy. Since then, many Ashia graduates have been and are running their own salons in the UK and abroad. Ashia Salon, open every day except Sunday, employs seven full-time stylists, three of whom are specialists in braiding and weave-on extensions.

Mrs Koroma is the daughter of the celebrated Accra trader Mami Yaa. The title of the evening, "Akwaaba", means "welcome" in Akan, one of the languages of Ghana.

Event Menu

The Akwaaba Dancers of The Beauty of Africa Show held at the Hammersmith

Ashia at the Caribbean's Elderly Rest Home with MP Kate Hoey.

Annual Kente Attire and Cultural Dance Competition

<u>Ashia and Daughter at Annual Kente Attire and Cultural Dance Competition, At the Clapham Common Hall</u>

Miss Ghana

Ashia with Miss Ghana winner at the Clapham common Hall Dance.

Ashia Cobblah

Victorine's 21st Birthday Party

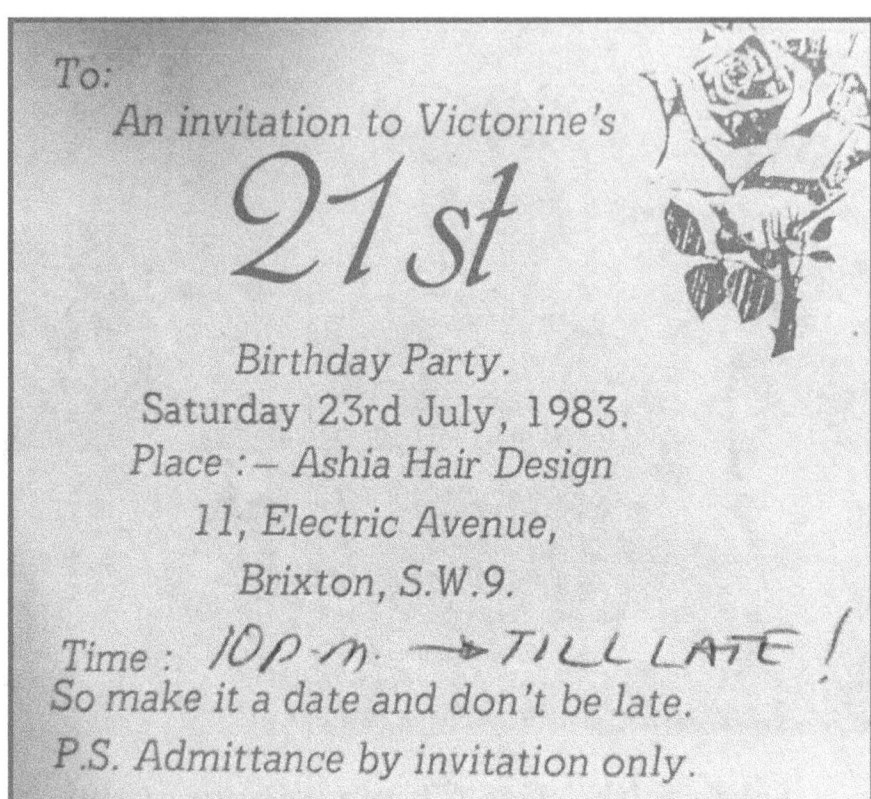

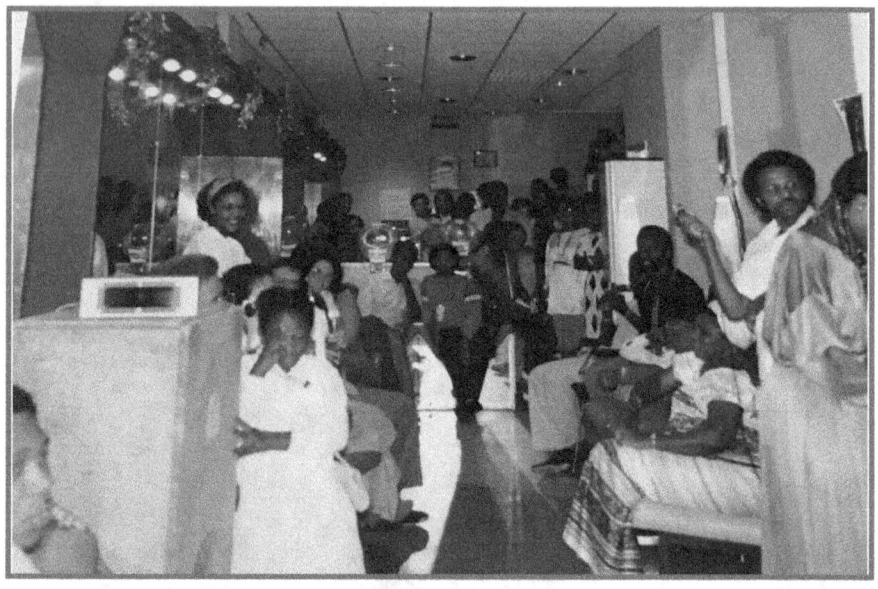

Victorine's 21st birthday held in the salon, it was on 2 floors, and it was a happy occasion.

Some Favourite Highlights:

Mrs. St Clair's Visit

One day at the salon, Mrs. St. Clair, surprised me with a visit and congratulated me on my business. I was really touched. I was in tears in front of the whole salon staff. I introduced her as *'my mother in the business'* who trained me to be good at my job.

At The Royal Albert Hall with Miss Ghana

One Saturday evening, the salon team and I were invited to The Royal Albert Hall to accompany Miss Ghana to watch the Miss World Pageant. It was an exciting weekend at South Kensington.

Chapter 41

The opening of The Ashia Hairdressing School

In 1983, after Victorine graduated as a hair and beauty lecturer from the world-renowned Pivot Point International School, we finally opened The School of Arts and Hairdressing on the first floor for awaiting students.

**Graduation day with Guest and Speaker-
The renowned Mr. Winston Issacs**

Our school was recognised both in the US and the UK. We were a member of Pivot Point International Schools, The World Federation of Hairdressing & Beauty Schools (WFHBS) and Hairdressing Council (HC) which was a statutory body established by an Act of Parliament. As we dealt with international learners, the UK Immigrations recognised and approved the school for visas to be issued to prospective students from various countries. Apart from students coming from Africa and the Caribbean, we had students from different parts of Europe. It was a busy time for us as we were training up to a dozen students at a time.

From The Gold Coast To Electric Avenue

SCENE

MOVING UP A CLASS...

AFRO hairdressing is a major growth area yet most hairdressers who work with European hair remain nervous of the subject. Not only are they unfamiliar with Afro hairdressing products they know very little about the structure of Afro hair and what its creative possibilities are.

This is largely the fault of existing training courses run by schools and privately-owned salons, who with a few notable exceptions do not cover the ins and outs of Afro and Asian hair.

Yet can any progressive, business-minded salon really afford to ignore the artistic and financial opportunities these clients present in 1985? Up to about six years ago there were hardly any good places to learn about this, but times have changed.

Good training does now exist on full and part-time basis, both for total beginners, *and* for experienced European hair stylists who want to find out more about any or all aspects of Afro hair work, so they can offer a more comprehensive service to clients. As yet, most places are in London or the South East, and recently several new editions to the Afro hairdressing education portfolio have started.

● **ASHIA HAIR & DESIGN**
1 Electric Avenue, Brixton,
London SW9
(01-274 1612).
ASHIA'S School is run by Victorine Koroma, and is affiliated to both the Caribbean/Afro Society of Hairdressers (CASH), the Hairdressers Council and National Hairdressers Federation. Its been running for three years and can be found above the Ashia salon in Brixton.

There are several courses available, the longest being a 36-week beginner's one which covers just about everything a foundation course could: product knowledge, trichology, precision hair cutting by the *Pivot Point* method (the salon is a franchise of Pivot Point) hair conditioning treatments, blow-drying, the use of curling irons, long hair work, relaxing, blow-outs (a semi-relax for a natural-looking effect) perms, colouring techniques, client relations *and* "international" hair, such as Chinese and Asian looks. That costs the student £1,400 (which includes £400 worth of equipment, and a Pivot Point voucher to the value of £700 for advanced Pivot Point course in Chicago).

"We can also customise courses for an individual's requirements, say for a hairdresser well trained with European hair only, who wanted to find out about, say, relaxing, perming and colouring Afro hair. The cost for that varies according to the client's requirements."

● **EBONY OF MAYFAIR,**
40 Priory Queensway, Birmingham / 18a Maddox St, London W1.
EBONY runs courses at both the above addresses, holding the beginners' ones in Birmingham with the advanced and certificate courses in London.

The certificate series (costing £575 inc VAT) helps delegates bone up on the areas where their knowledge is weakest, but participants need to know the basics of Afro hairdressing.

Syllabus varies according to delegates' requirements and lasts eight weeks. The one week courses may be suitable for a trained European hair stylist who wants to look at some of the most popular Afro hair areas, as it zones on a limited number of subjects, again chosen by those on the course. Tuition costs £149 inc VAT.

Beginners (diploma) courses cover Afro and European hair therapy but most of the practical work is carried out on Afro heads. Subjects dealt with include cutting, colouring, perming, relaxing, trichology, bacteriology, pH analysis, weaving, iron curling, crimping, working with long hair, braiding, extensions, twisting, weave-ons... and health safety. There's room in the classes for a maximum of 20 people, full/part-time students are both welcomed, and the course costs £975.60 inc VAT.

Ebony is able to arrange inexpensive accommodation in Birmingham from around £25 per week. The company has taught students ever since it opened. "There was so much demand, we had no choice," says co-owner Evonne Williams. The fully fledged school above their Birmingham salon has been open for two years and Birmingham Ebony is also an agent for YTS, and its students do not have to attend college on top of salon practice, (Manpower Services Commission reckon they are being taught everything they need where they are!)

● **LONDON COLLEGE OF FASHION,**
Specialist College, 20 John Princess Street, London W1
(01-629 9401).
THE College is best known for its fashion, art and design students — and of course, its European hairdressing courses but it is also launching an Afro hair course this autumn. The course is aiming it at those "who have only had experience with European hair and who wish to extend their repertoire."

It covers "all aspects" of Afro work: hair types, growth, product usage, relaxing, re-arranging, dressing, and client education. It last two terms for one afternoon and one evening per week (Mondays 4pm to 9pm), costs around £60, is limited to groups of 12 to 14 people and is a mix of lectures, practical and demo work.

Prospective students must have finished a salon apprenticeship or a full-time hairdressing course, and preferably be working within the industry.

● **MACS SCHOOL OF HAIRDRESSING,**
309 Railton Road, London E24 (01-733 2219).
MACS run seven-to-eight-month Beginners courses or shorter refresher variations which may be suitable for both experienced Afro and European-hair stylists

Morris Masterclass' new Afro school in London's West End

Publications of my Salon & school, "Moving up a Class"

The great thing about having a school connected to a salon was that the students could assist and work alongside experienced stylists and get practical experience from the salon.

Ashia with International Students at their Graduation

Ella, a Salon Owner from France, graduated from an advanced Hairdressing course

The courses were awarded by recognised bodies, with diplomas and certificates covering all aspects of hairdressing. We had a graduation ceremony every year for students who had completed their courses. A lot of our students returned to their country of origin to set-up hairdressing businesses through our advice and guidance. We were able to supply them with equipment and products.

The Hairdressing School Prospectus

Hairdressing School merger

Mr. Enoch Williams approached us for the possibility of joining his Ebony School of Hairdressing with our school. Mr. Williams was a popular figure in both the community and the industry. He was also the owner of the Ultimate Hair Salon located on the first floor above the Brixton station and the manufacturer of Single Bible hair product range. It was an honor to be connected with him. Brixton underground had issued a notice of expansion, so businesses had to relocate. Consequently, in 1987, Mr. William's hairdressing school and ours merged to become Ashia Ebony School of Hairdressing.

Chapter 42

The Belgium Students Visit

Belgium Students with teachers visit the Ashia Ebony School Students, Mr Williams stood on the right-hand side, 1986

Belgium Students visiting Ashia Hair Salon with staff and students, with our PR, Jane Hammond beside Ashia & Belgium Delegate (2nd from the left) & Victorine

We received a request from an Institute in Antwerp, 'Technisch Instituut Sint Maria' asking if they could visit with their students to learn about afro hair as part of their week in London. It was an unusual request so we discussed it with our public relations officer,

Jane Hammond. She agreed that it would be an exciting collaboration. So, we agreed to the request. I forgot to ask how they knew about us.

In April 1986, the first group of 13 students and 2 teachers arrived for an educational day. It was a fun day. After the visit, it became a yearly program.

.

Chapter 43

The opening of The Wholesale Business

After opening a wholesale business in the basement, selling various items: products, equipment and educational books, it became a success. I eventually employed two men to run that area of business on behalf of Ashia Hair Design.

One of the men was my childhood friend from Ghana who I met at a function. He told me he was unemployed and needed help so I decided to offer him the position of wholesale manager.

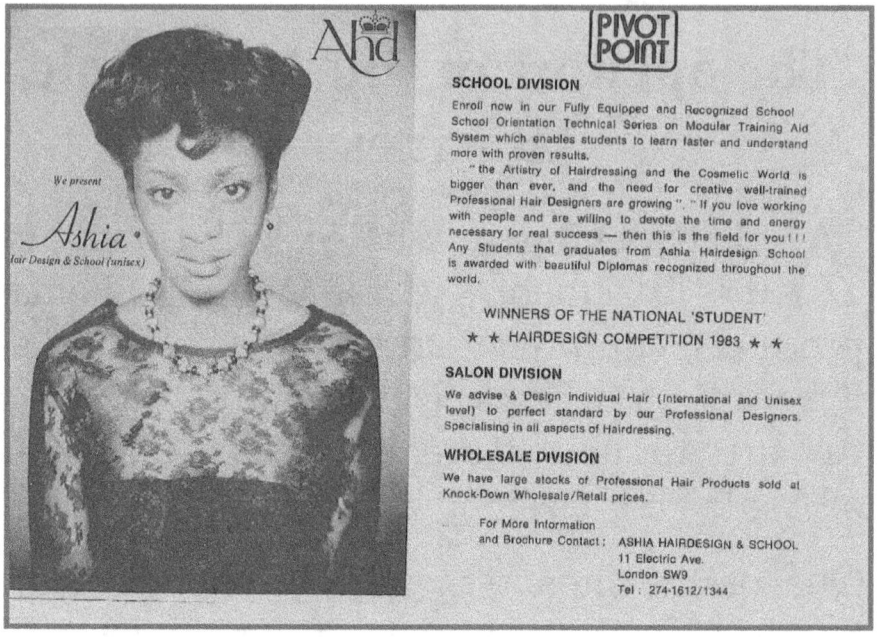

A magazine feature of the three Salon divisions

Apart from supplying salon equipment and products to our graduate students, we also supply to other salons and hairdressers across England and abroad who had also started selling goods made in Ghana and parts of Asia. We were also selling traditional African wear and fur jackets. Italian leather-goods and textile cloths from Holland had also become lucrative. We also helped a few local sole-traders to sell their goods.

Chapter 44

My Retirement

After a long career in the beauty industry, I retired in 1994. My daughter was now married to a Doctor and I was hoping for my first grandchild. They are currently pursuing their own future.

What a journey it had been, to have fulfilled a life goal! Owning a hairdressing salon business that became a three-floor empire and to have succeeded in helping my family, friends and others were my wonderful legacies.

Ashia Cobblah

My daughter, Victorine and I, 2016

I am truly grateful. Now that I am retired and become a senior citizen, I have all the time to attend church and the freedom to travel around the world. I am fulfilled and happy spending time with my grandchildren, family and friends.

Enjoying time with a friend in Ghana

Visiting A Friend In Germany.

Ashia, on her retirement, completes one of her goals to visit Israel, Jerusalem.

Ashia attending a function in the U.K

Chapter 45

The Ashia Benevolent Foundation (ABF)

In 1981, I was on a visit to Ghana for the first time in several years. I visited my family's church, Sacred Heart Parish. During the church service, it was announced that they will be celebrating their 30th Anniversary and they required a donation for new robes for the choir. I decided to contribute. This was the beginning and an opportunity for my journey to 'give back'.

A few years later, I was reflecting on the communities in the villages in Togo where my father came from. I recalled on one visit to the churches that the choir did not have or wear robes. I decided to donate robes to the churches as well. On my trip to Ghana, I decided to get robes for them.

Donated Choir Robes to Churches in Togo

I thought about the three small communities in Togo with five churches, I decided to donate twenty robes per church.

Donated Choir Robes to Church's in Togo

I also remembered the vulnerable, the elderly and the children. When I was travelling to Ghana and Togo, I brought bundles of clothes from London which was distributed to them.

I made school uniforms and provided books for selected children in need and also paid school fees for them.

SAINT CECILIA CHOIR
SACRED HEART PARISH
Box 1747 • Tel. No. 64218
ACCRA, GHANA

1st July 1982.

Mrs Florence Koroma,
Porden Road,
London S.W.2,
England.

Dear Madam

<u>THANK YOU:</u>

The Executive and the entire members of the above named Choir wish to render their sincere thanks for your kind donation of ₵800.00 towards the purchase of our new choir robes.

It will interest you to hear that the robes which were ordered from the U.S.A. arrived on time for the Choir's 30th anniversary which fell on 22nd November 1981.

We are most grateful to you, and hope that this relationship between us will find Christ at the centre of it to direct and control all affairs between us to the glory of God the Almighty.

May the good Lord, bless and reward you abundantly in all your endeavours.

Yours In-Christ,

F. A. EWOOL
(PRESIDENT)

A letter of Thanks from The Sacred Heart Parish, Ghana 1982

The Archbishop of Accra Most Rev. Dominic K Andoh

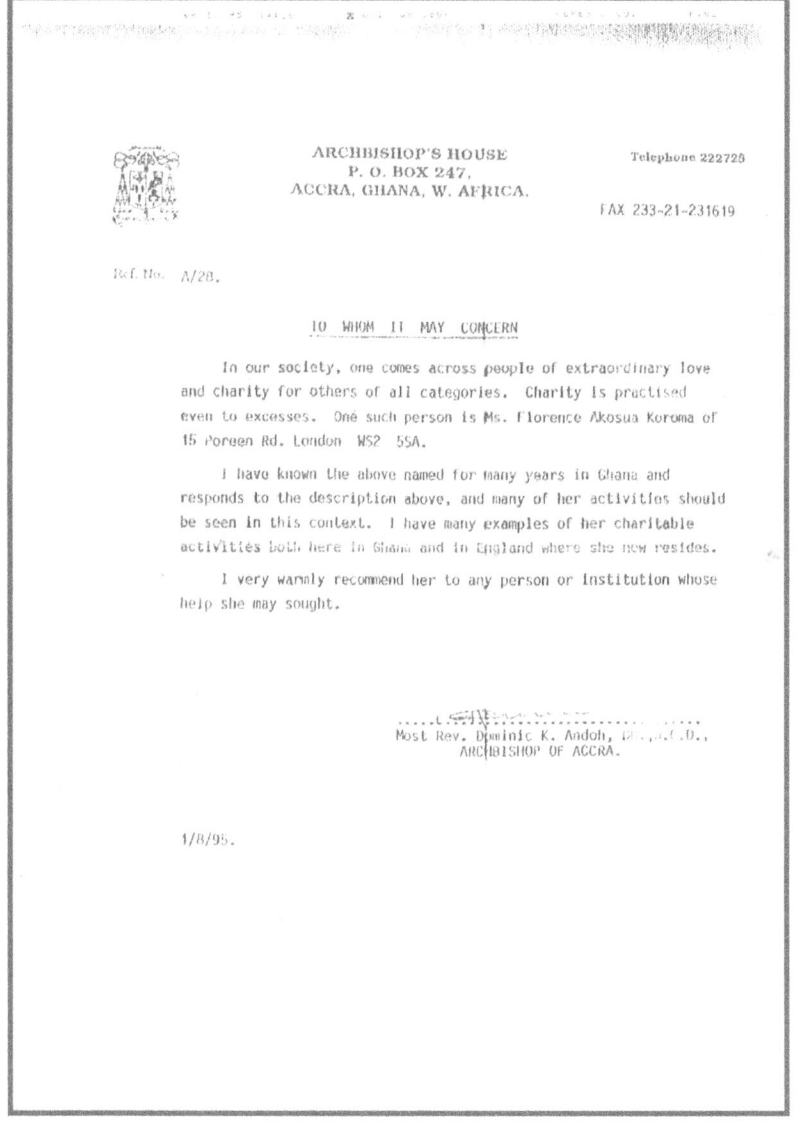

A Letter from The Archbishop's House, The Archbishop of Accra Most Rev. Dominic K. Andoh

As I am now retired, I have decided to set up a private foundation, Ashia Benevolent Foundation to continue helping the vulnerable: The elderly, young single mothers, children and the church.

<u>A visit to greet Rev. Father A. Kretschmer at The Holy Spirit Cathedral-Accra, Ghana</u>

When I retired, I decided to set up a private foundation- Ashia Benevolent Foundation- to continue to help the vulnerable: the elderly, young single mothers, children and the church.

Chapter 46

Poultry and Event business venture in Ghana

After I retired from the beauty business in London, I decided to spend time in Ghana with my family and friends and to take things easy and at a slower pace.

Few weeks later in Ghana, I got bored and wanted to do something. I realised there were no chicken farms in the area and as I loved eating eggs for breakfast, I spoke with my sisters and they agreed and we decided to set up a poultry business, raising chickens and selling the eggs within the family house since it was vast.

Our poultry Farm in Accra, Ghana.

We hired two assistants and within a month we created a chicken farm, bought a few male and female chickens, and the business was started. We supplied eggs to businesses and sold chickens. Within a short time, we became known in the area and that was how the business took off.

Few months later, we became successful and were swamped with orders. We later discovered that some neighbors had set-up copycat operations. I was happy to be an inspiration.

Event Equipment Hire Service

In Ghana, there were always a lot of functions to attend: baby dedications, weddings, birthday celebrations and funerals. I used to attend a lot of them. I realized there was not a lot of businesses that rented event equipment so I started the business of providing function canopies, chairs and tables as well as plates and cutleries and other items.

Finally, I hope to come out with a sequel to this book about my journey of tribulation and spiritual experiences.

Chapter 47

Some Popular Produce from Ghana and the Continent

Apart from the Gold, Cocoa, timber and spices, especially the "Grains of Paradise."

Akpeteshie: (ak-PEH-teh-she) is traditional liquor distilled from the palm tree or sugar cane. It is the strongest type of drink for the brave-hearted.

Asaana: is a non-alcoholic and sweet drink made from crushed, fermented corn and sugar, a favorite drink around town. It is brown in color and served with ice. A staple at functions: Weddings, Baby dedications, Birthday parties and funerals.

Bamboo: people are surprised that there are bamboos in Africa. It is used to make sustainable domestic produce, furniture and bicycles. It is also used as part of building structures.

Baobab: is a pod that grows on a gigantic prehistoric tree. Its powdery content of the pod is used for fruit juice and porridge.

It is very popular in the north of Ghana and Togo and surrounding areas. It has been scientifically tested and is nutrient-dense with health properties. It has been recognized for its health benefits around the world.

Basket weaves: we are talented in creating designs of baskets and bags. They are now seen and exported across the world.

Calabash bowls and jugs: from a plant that we dry and smooth out, which we use as; drink and water carriers, drinking cups and bowls to eat. I believe this must be the first drinking and eating containers for mankind before the use of wineskins and glass and porcelain.

Coconut: from the coconut tree, we have extracted: oil for skin and for cooking and the water for drinking. It has now been known in Europe and globally as a very healthy alternative to milk and used for moisturizing skin.

Cocoa Butter: obtained from the cocoa beans after fermentation. It has several uses; popularly used to make chocolates, Beauty products; toiletries and also pharmaceutical uses.

Clay bowls and pots: we have been designing and creating clay bowls and plates to eat and pots for cooking for centuries.

Dental sticks and sponges: Got from the Neem tree and the Salvadora persica tree. This is our very effective tooth and mouth cleaner from ancient times

Grains of Paradise: Is locally known as alligator pepper. It has a distinct flavor between black pepper, cloves and ginger used in culinary dishes and alcoholic beverages. It has become a worldwide popular seasoning.

Honey: This is the most popular sweetener known since ancient times. It is used in drinks, beauty products and medicines. What is most unique about honey is the fact that it does not get spoiled, even after thousands of years.

Kola nuts: Got from the Kola tree. It has a bitter flavor and contains caffeine. From the ancient times, it was chewed by the Kings, Chiefs and elders and is usually presented to guests in private, social and ceremonial settings. It is also medicinal; aiding in digestion and also as a cough mixture when grounded and mixed with honey. Globally, kola has been used as a flavoring ingredient for cola drinks.

Moringa: Got from the Moringa Oleifa tree and commonly known as the 'Miracle tree' because of its drought-resistant nature. It is a fast growing and perennial plant. Every part of the tree is valuable, from the roots, bark, flowers, seeds and the leaves. The leaves are found to be nutrient-dense. We have been using the leaves in salads and drinks since ancient times.

Moringa has been scientifically tested and has been confirmed to have superior qualities and abundance of nutrients in comparison to other health vegetation. It has become very popular around the world.

Palm Oils: extracted from the palm nuts and

palm kernels. There are two types of oils we produce: Red oil and light color oil, which we use in cooking. In Europe, Palm oils are used in beauty cosmetics and in the food industry.

Palm Wine: We extract two types of liquid from the palm tree, which is then fermented to make a white-colored wine popularly known as 'Palmie'. In the olden days it was known as Dr. White.

Pito: A favorite drink served warm or cold. It is made from fermented millet or sorghum. It is a popular strong alcoholic drink in the North of Ghana.

Shea Butter: is prized and has become worldwide popular produce of Ghana and other neighboring countries. It has become very lucrative, used in cosmetics and beauty products around the world. It is one of the oldest products that have been scientifically proven to contain healthy and nutritious properties. Around parts of Ghana, it is used for cooking.

Sobol: A sweet and healthy drink made from

Hibiscus leaves, also known as 'Bissap'.

Sugar Cane: we cultivate to make sugar, drinks and desserts. We extract the juice to create alcohol beverages. It is a very popular export for sugar since the 18th century.

Wood Carving: we are also talented artists in wood carvings from ancient times. The arts have now got a global market in some reputable auction houses around the world.

Chapter 48

Some Popular African Proverbs and Pearls of Wisdom

During Ancient times, Africans had always used proverbs to advise, educate and inspire. They were philosophical sayings that forced you to think, to reflect and to ponder. We take proverbs seriously because they usually came from our grandparents and the elders of our communities and are passed down through generations. They are always figurative in nature.

"Evhe Proverbs, their origin, relevance and philosophy are based in the sociocultural education of the Evhes"-Padmore Agbemabiese.

In recent times, quotes have become a popular form of proverbs globally. Below are some favorite proverbs out of millions.

"A single tree cannot make a forest" ~**Evhe: Ghana, Togo.**

A single tree refers to an influential, prominent, elderly or wealthy person in a society, e.g. a king, president or a chief. The forest also refers to an institution, family or community. The proverb, therefore, depicts a rich or prominent person alone cannot constitute a family, region, state or nation. There are forest areas in the Evhe land, and during the farming season, it calls for the communal spirit and teamwork.

"Though the earth is solid, the Chameleon makes cautious steps on it" ~ **Ghanaian, Togolese** - (The earth being solid indicates that life is complicated and full of challenges, and the chameleon refers to the people on the earth and therefore they should move according to the earth formation or life's situation.)

"Two calabashes floating on the water usually touch each other" ~ **Ghana/ Togo** (The calabash means friendship and family set-up in the society or community, whereas water refers to the cordial relationship between family and friends. Therefore, the interrelationship that binds the parties together should solve or address all frictions between them with tactfulness.)

"Until the lion has his or her own storyteller, the hunter will always have the best part of the story"-**Benin, Ghana, Togo Proverbs**

The interesting thing about African Proverbs is the variants in different African languages, which show their own inter-connections. Examples of such variants are:

"Until lions have their own historians, tales of the hunt shall always glorify the hunter" ~ **Nigeria**.

"Until lions start to write down their own stories, the hunters will always be the heroes." ~ **Kenya and Zimbabwe**.

I have learnt the importance and love for the whole of the continent of Africa through the quotes from President Kwame Nkrumah about unity.

Here are lists of some popular proverbs from Africa in alphabetical order:

"Even the colours of a chameleon are for

survival not beauty. ~ **African Proverbs**

"A sensible enemy is better than a narrow-minded friend." ~ **Algeria**

"Beautiful words don't put porridge in the pot." ~ **Botswana**

"Every birth is the rebirth of an ancestors" ~ **Burkina Faso**

"An elephant does not get tired carrying his trunk" ~ **Burundi**

"The heart of the wise man lies quiet like limpid water ~**Cameroon**.

"Whoever tells the truth is chased out of nine villages" ~ **Capo Verde**.

"You are beautiful; but learn to work, for you cannot eat your beauty" ~ **Central African Republic**.

"The lion's power lies in our fear of him" ~ **Chad**

"We can win a woman with lies, but you cannot feed her with lies" ~ **Comoros Islands**

"Wisdom is like fire. People take it from

others" ~ **Democratic Republic of Congo**.

"A woman's strength is a multitude of words" ~ **Djibouti**

"The best and shortest road towards knowledge of truth is Nature" ~**Egypt**

"Coffee and love taste best when hot" ~ **Ethiopia**

"I'm still patient until patience gets tired of me" ~ **Eritrea**

"A wise man never knows all, only fools know everything" ~ **Equatorial Guinea**

"Bad friends will prevent you from having good friends" ~**Gabon**

"Before healing others, heal yourself" ~ **Gambia**

"Wisdom is like a baobab tree; no one individual can embrace it ~**Ghana**

"Knowledge without wisdom is like water in the sand" ~**Guinea**

"By the time the fool has learned the game, the players have dispersed" ~ **Guinea Bissau**.

"Mutual affection gives each his share"
~**Ivoire Coast**

"A man who uses force is afraid of reasoning"
~ **Kenya**

"A fight between grasshoppers is a joy to the crow" ~ **Lesotho**

"A little rain each day will fill the rivers to overflowing" ~ **Liberia**

"Women were born to be treasured" ~**Libya**

"Advice is a stranger; if he's welcome he stays for the night; if not, he leaves the same day ~ **Malagasy (Madagascar)**

"He who thinks he is leading and has no one following him is only taking a walk" ~ **Malawi**.

"A person doesn't give without a motive" ~ **Mali**

"Bad leaders are elected by poor citizens who don't vote" ~ **Mauritania**

"Not all the flowers of a tree produces fruit" ~**Mauritius**

"Instruction in youth is like engraving in stone" ~ **Morocco**

"Witch doctors do not sell their potions to each other" ~ **Mozambique**.

"Learning expands great souls" ~**Namibia**.

"There is no medicine against old age" ~ **Niger**

"It is the rainy season that gives wealth" ~ **Nigeria**.

"Happiness can grow from only a little contentment" ~ Pigmy (Aka, Efe, Mbuti people) **Central Africa**

"A friend who visits you when you are suffering is your best friend" ~ **Rwanda**

"A thief passes for a gentleman stealing has made him rich" ~ **Sao Tome/Principe**

"There can be no peace without understanding ~ **Senegal**

"He who looks for honey must have the courage to face the bees" ~ **Seychelles**

"If the cockroach wants to rule over the

chicken, then it must hire the fox as a bodyguard" ~ **Sierra Leone**

"Wisdom does not come overnight" ~ **Somalia**.

"A large chair does not make a king" ~ **Sudan**

"Knowledge is like a lion; it cannot be gently embraced" ~ **South African**

"The bee that is forced into the hive will not produce the honey" ~ **Swaziland**

"A wise person will always find a way" ~ **Tanzania**.

"No one tests the depth of a river with both feet" ~ **Togo**

"He who is covered with other people's clothes is naked" ~ **Tunisia**

"By trying often, the monkey learns to jump from the tree ~ **Uganda (Buganda)**

"A ripened fruit does not cling to the vine"~**Zimbabwe.**

Source: Alexkpodonulibrary.com, Afritorial, Eritrean quote from Alamin Abdullatif

www.ingramcontent.com/pod-product-compliance
Lightning Source LLC
Chambersburg PA
CBHW081227080526
44587CB00022B/3852